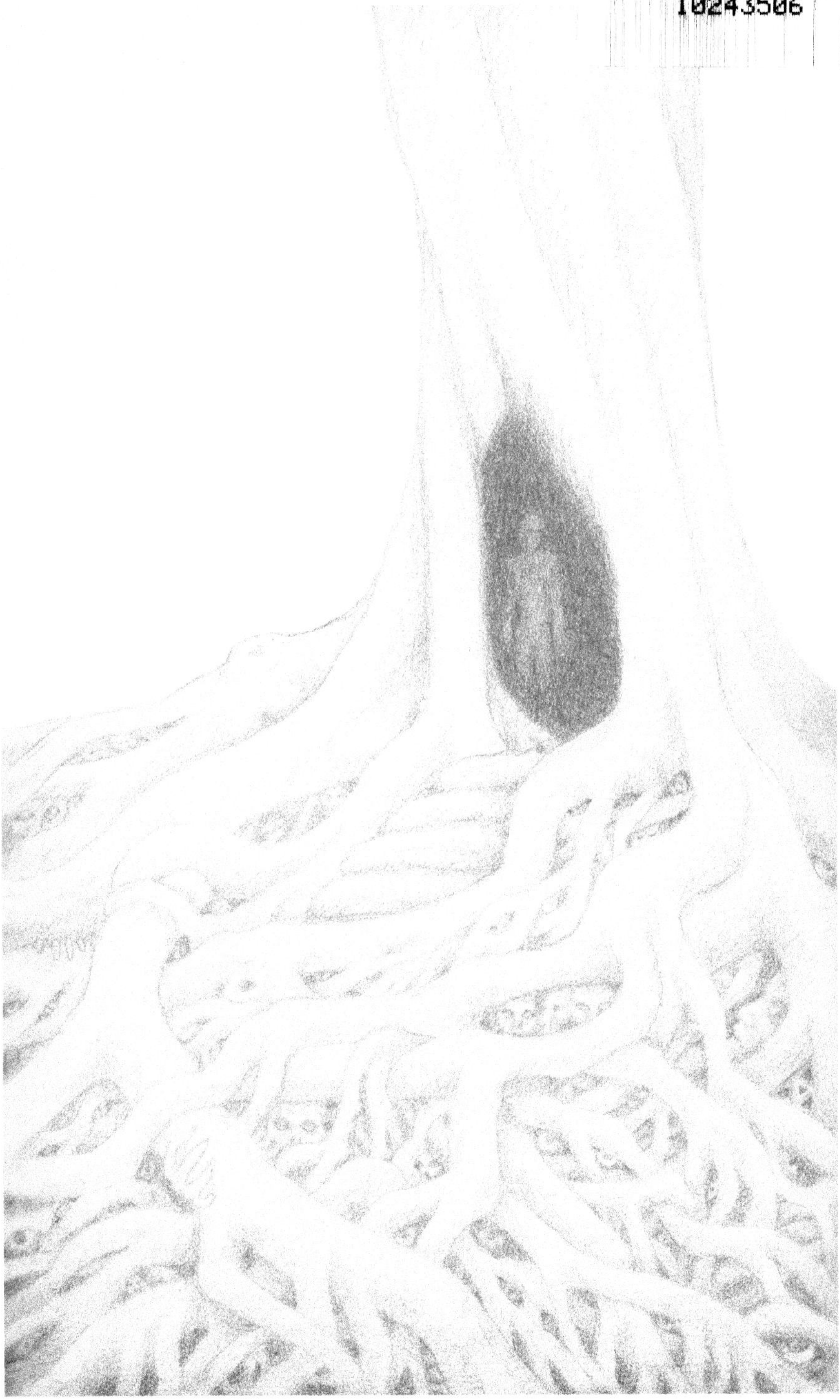

This book is dedicated to the Ancestors.
Those who came before us, those who come after us,
and blood that links us all together.

Frontispiece: *Apparition* by Amanda Manesis

UNDER WORLD

SHAMANISM
MYTH
MAGICK

CHRIS ALLAUN

Copyright © Christopher Allaun 2022

All rights reserved. No reproduction, copy or transmission of this publication may be made without written permission. No paragraph of this publication may be reproduced, copied or transmitted without permission or in accordance with the provision of the copyright act of 1956 (as amended).

Cover art/design Amanda Manesis www.amaradulcis.com

Other works by Chris Allaun
Deeper into the Underworld: Death, Ancestors & Magical Rites
Upperworld: Shamanism and Magick of the Celestial Realms

Contents

Preface to the Revised Edition 7

Introduction 10

1   Underworld 20

The Psychological Underworld and the Mind; Creation of the Underworld; Why go to the Underworld?; Odin's Sacrifice (Norse); Mapping the Underworld; Time and Space; Entrances into the Underworld; The Planes of Existence; P; Astral Projection and Shamanic Journeying; Finding Your Spirit Animal; Finding your Underworld Guide.

2   Navigating the Underworld 50

The Descent of Ishtar ; Entering The Underworld; Landscapes; Places of Oracles; Realm of the Dead; Beginning Your Underworld Journey; Where The Dead Live; The Spirit Wife (Native American Zuni); Hades/Elysian Fields; Hel, The Nordic World of the Dead; The Celtic Otherworld/Underworld; Anwyyn; The Celtic Islands of the Otherworld; Exercise: Exploring the Underworld; Place of Rejuvenation; Exercise: Finding Your Underworld Place of Healing; The Six Bardos.

3   The Hell Worlds 98

The Hells; The Maya; Beliefs; Road to Xibalba; One and Seven Hanahpu; Hanahpu and Xblanque in the Underworld; Egyptian Underworld; Osiris and Isis (Egyptian); Chronology; The Egyptian Soul; Trials and Monsters; Apophis; Joining the Gods in Dwat; Christian Hell; My Personal Experience in Hell; Qliphoth; Creation of the Qliphoth; Personal Hell and Fears; Exercise:

4   Creatures of the Underworld 153

Kali Ma (Hindu); Things That Lurk in Dark Places; Parasites/ Attachments/Larvae; Lost Souls; Dwarves; Dark Elves; Guardians; Wisdom Keepers; Vampires; Demons; Demons and the Ceremonial Magician; On Demons and Gods; The Sleeping Gods and the Old Ones; Dragons; Gods and Goddesses.

5   Those Who Stay Behind 176

Herne the Hunter (Welsh); Why the Dead Come to Visit; Proper Burial; To Speak of the Afterlife and Underworld; Unfinished Business; Forgiveness ; Becoming Spirit Guides and Helpers; Preparing Us for Death; Ritual to Help Spirits Cross Over; The Burial If There Is No Body; Helping The Dead Out of Their Own Traps; Suicide and Unfinished Business; Helping the Dead Trapped by Repressed Beliefs; Helping Spirits Cross Over; Hauntings; Our Grief Binds Spirits to this World; Valediction.

Bibliography 213

Index 218

Preface to the Revised Edition

Underworld was published five years ago and many things have changed since then. I've changed a lot since then. *Underworld* was my first book to be published and as I look back on these five years I see that I was blessed by the gods to be able to share my work and experiences with the world. This book opened up many doors for me. I have been able to meet so many people, both in person and online, who resonated with the energies of the worlds that are "below" us. Before *Underworld* came out in 2016 there were no books available that dealt exclusively with the subterranean shamanic realm. You could find a few pages here and there in shamanic books but never a whole book dedicated to this fascinating place. I spoke with so many people who were inspired by this book and incorporated the teachings and techniques into their own spiritual practice.

The world has changed so much in the last five years. Currently, as I write this we are still in the COVID pandemic. Many people have died and millions have become sick with the virus. With so much death in the world right now I thought that now is the time to create a Revised Edition of *Underworld*. The world needs Spirit Walkers and Healers to heal the wounds that have been inflicted not just on the earth but on our fellow humans as well. We need to journey into the Underworld and face our demons in order to find wholeness and balance. This is the time.

I have developed my writing style a great deal in the last five years. I have published five books so far and how I write and relay information and magick has evolved. For the better I hope. As I revised this book I did my best to maintain the style of writing that captured the imaginations of so many people. At the same time, I modernized some of the writing as well as kept the idea of appropriation in mind. I have Cherokee blood in my veins but I study under Lakota teachers. Here in Chicago there are several Lakota spiritual groups in the surrounding area who I have had the blessings to work with and share in community. That being said, I rewrote some things such as "Totem" which is an Ojibway word and replaced it with the term "Spirit Animal". I don't practice Ojibway so I thought it best to change the world to something a little more universal.

People have asked me over the years why I chose to add Native American stories to my books. The answer is two fold. Native American teachings are a part of my spirituality and they are sacred stories that teach us how to better human beings. Secondly, many Native American reservations are suffering. There is so much poverty, suicide, and health problems on the reservations and no one seems to care. Or maybe my readers don't know. My goal is to share the beauty of some of the Native American culture so people will begin to see the value of these wonderful people and the healing they give the earth. Maybe then people will start to donate to the reservations or charities who help the people of the reservations.

My talented friend John Hijatt took the manuscript and did some wonderful editing with it. There were many things that were missed last time around that I wanted to fix. When an author writes a book we might read it 1000 times. Our brains tend to miss things such as grammar and sentence structure. This is why it was a goddess-send to have John take another look at the book for me and correct mistakes that were made the first time around. Thank you so much John!

If this is your first time entering the Underworld you will be going on a fantastic adventure into the depths of the Universe and even your subconscious mind. If you read the first edition of *Underworld* then you are in for a treat with this revision. Close your eyes. Take a deep breath and find yourself in the world of the ancestors, demons, and adventure....

    Chris Allaun
    Autumn Equinox 2021

Introduction

The Underworld is a place of magick and power. Most of us, when we are learning magick and spiritual wisdom seek the four elements, the world around us, and the stars above. All of these things do, indeed, hold power. But what of the world below? There is a vast world beneath us that many fear. Shamans, witches, and magicians know that the Underworld has many secrets. The Underworld, to many, is dark and a place of monsters and the sinful dead. It can certainly be that, but there is much more to be revealed.

Some of us are taught that the Underworld is a place of devils and tortured souls. A place to stay away from at all costs. Yes, there are such places, such as the Greco-Roman Tartarus that keeps the Titans chained up in the depths, but these are only a small portion of the Underworld. The Underworld is also a place of healing, rejuvenation, and ancient wisdom. In the Nordic Myths we have the Well of Mimir. Mimir is a god who's severed head was placed in a well, giving out prophecies and oracles to all who would dare enter. There is also the land of the ancestors. This is a place where our loved ones dwell after death. In some myths, they are protected by the Nordic goddess, Hel (Hela), in others, by Hades and Persephone.

The Underworld is also a place to find spirits to heal the sick and protect our community. There are spirits who teach us how to cure disease and rid ourselves of the dark spirits who try to harm us. The Underworld is linked to our subconscious mind. Facing the mysteries of the depths can help us understand our innermost fears and the shadows of our own mind. It is taught that the energies of the Underworld are frightening only when we allow fear, hate, and regret to keep us from awakening to our spiritual path. When we journey into places we fear, we are able to face our "personal monsters". We have all heard the saying, "where there is fear there is power". This is part of the ordeal each of us must face. In Egyptian mythology, the sun god Ra, must take his nightly journey into the Underworld. Each night he faces the monster Apophis, who tries to destroy the sun barge and kill Ra. Each night, Ra defeats the monster and is able to give the Egyptian people the healing light of the sun once more.

I have worked with the Underworld for many years. I have seen some of the most dark and odd places and yet I have also seen some of the most beautiful things. To me, the Underworld is the healing place for our ancestors. The Realm of the Dead is peaceful, beautiful, and serene. It is here that our loved ones are protected and cared for by many great healing spirits and deities. Our ancestors have many things to teach us. They can also help us with things related to family and genetic diseases that stem from blocked energy. One of the most rewarding parts of my spiritual practice is communing with the ancestors.

But what of those dark places? What of the monsters that hide within the caves and caverns? There are certainly spirits that do not wish us well. The deep caverns of the Underworld are the resting place of the Titans, the chthonic gods who cause destruction and chaos to our world. It is also the place where, Fenrir, the giant wolf is chained so that he cannot bring the end of days. There are also chthonic spirits who some call demons who seek destruction. Yet, I have found these spirits to be more chaotic than "evil". When we face our demons we release the chaotic energy back into the depths, freeing the magick inside of us.

In my travels to the Underworld, I have discovered that it is a place of great healing and power. Both the dark and the light have great things to teach. You may be wondering why it is important to face the dark? The dark times in our lives are when we grow the most. When we face adversity and challenges, we must decide if we stay complacent and suffer, or do we face the challenge and allow ourselves to become more than we are now. The mystery is, of course, who is it that we become? Do we embrace the darkness? Or do we stay in ignorant bliss in the light?

I have a story told to me by one of my teachers:

Before there was fire everyone was cold. There was no sacred bonfire. There were no sacred torches to light the way. During the night all was dark and so very cold. The animals had a great meeting to figure out what to do. They said, "Who will find heat and light for us? Who will help us?"

The little mouse said, "There is a volcano that goes way deep in the earth. I will go there and get fire." So, the little mouse ran to the mouth of the volcano. He peered in and saw fire and great spirits that made thunderous noise. "The underneath is too frightening. I cannot go down there. I will surely die!"

After the mouse came back empty handed, the animal council asked again. "Who will find heat and light for us?"

The adder said, "I will go into the volcano for us!" So, the adder slithered to the mouth of the volcano. As he peered down, he saw the brightness of the lava and said, "The light is too bright and too hot. I will surely die if I go there."

The adder came back empty handed, and the animal council asked again. "Who will find heat and light for us?"

Finally, the crow said, "I have a magical bag and I can fly. I will go into the volcano and get heat and light for us." So, the crow took his magical bag and flew to the mouth of the volcano. He saw the fire and the great thunderous spirits. He also saw the brightness of the lava. He had much fear but without hesitation he took flight! He flew down into the depths of the volcano. He flew down into the earth and there he found a hot coal and put it into his bag. He flew as fast as he could past the fires and the thunderous spirits. He brought one coal to the animal council. They rejoiced in his bravery. The placed the coal on the little wooden pile and this is how the first sacred fire was made

Shamanism, Myth, and Magick

The people of the tribe sat around the sacred campfire. The light and the heat from the flames was magical—the source of life. The tribe's Shaman, dressed in skins and bones, was about to tell the story of the dead. The people were hushed. No one dared speak. The shaman's words were magical: a spell for all those who listened. He began his tale about the young hero who left the peacefulness of the tribe to seek adventure. The shaman explained how the young man found himself deep beneath the Earth, surrounded by the dead. But the hero found the courage to journey forth in the subterranean lands. For days and days, the hero explored the strange lands. He saw many strange things. He saw creatures who were ancient and kept their magical secrets very close. He saw many strange things: lovely maidens who revealed themselves as old hags, landscapes that would shift into nothingness and then back again, and dark beings that crept about in the deep. But he also saw great places of beauty and healing. The Shaman went on to tell of the great demons that tried to kill the hero, but the hero prevailed. Eventually he confronted the darkest part of the depths. It was through this darkness that the hero found the true healing of his spirit and the wisdom needed for the survival of his tribe. "What was this wisdom?" the shaman asked with a dark laugh. "Journey into the Underworld and find out for yourself."

When the ancient people lived in tribes, they told stories around the fires to explain the world around them. These stories became myths, and these later became the foundation of religion. Myths are stories told to explain the forces of creation, life, death and what happens in the afterlife. When we look closely, we find that they are much more than simply stories told to people to explain natural phenomena, such as the rising sun, the moon overhead, or a terrible storm. Myths were designed in accordance with the energy of the spirits, or even the god or goddess they referred to. Myths were also told as a guide to the social structure of the tribe, village, or city. They tell the listener what was expected of them during their lifetime and after death. The hero's journey was common to all ancient cultures and civilizations. These stories showed what happened when he or she journeyed out of the safety of the village. Sometimes bad luck would fall, unfortunate occurrences that would lead the hero on a path of transformation.

Myths were crafted in such a way that they also spoke to the hopes, fears, and struggles of the everyday person. Because human beings have the same needs, we also have the same hopes, fears, and desires. If we compare myths from around the world, we can see many of the same themes repeating. Psychologist Carl Jung calls these "archetypes." A few examples of archetypes include "The Shaman", "The Villain", or "The Maiden." Let us take the example of The Shaman. The Shaman archetype includes all shamans that ever were and all shamans that ever will be. In many societies shamans were needed to journey into the spirit worlds to gain wisdom and power for the benefit of the tribe. Myths contained archetypes because the listener related to them. As the story was being told, it was possible for the listeners to see themselves as the shaman going on the adventure.

Myths have "spiritual truth" in them. Spiritual truth is not the same as dogma or stories that are to be taken literally. Shamans and other people who worked with the spirits used their psychic vision to observe the universe and their surroundings. Shamans teach through stories and myth. In tribal cultures, there are no books of spiritual laws or commandments to teach right and wrong. The lessons were taught in the tales of the shaman. It was up to each individual to take the stories and draw their own conclusion. When we are young and inexperienced, we understand the "surface" lesson of the myths. Later, as we grow spiritually, we discover a deeper meaning with the stories. We begin to relate to the hero's journey. When I was a child, I loved the stories of King Arthur and the Knights of the Round Table. I loved reading books and watching movies about Arthur and the wizard Merlin. It was not until I studied Paganism and spirituality that I began to understand the complexities and spiritual meanings of the King Arthur stories. To learn how King Arthur was magically connected to the land and how Avalon was a sacred place of the dead was rewarding and has had a lasting impression on me.

When we look closely at the myths of the Underworld, we can use them to create our own magick. Myths were more than just stories to the ancient peoples. It became part of their culture and spiritual practice. The story was often told in a ceremony that was designed to leave a powerful imprint on the seeker. In this way, the myths became a living part of spirituality. If we take the example of the Elysian Mysteries, the myth of the Rape and Descent of Persephone is woven into Greek spirituality. The priest would take the seeker down into the "Underworld" that was a temple dedicated to Hades and Persephone. It was there the myth was played out so that it would have a great impact on the seeker.

In many shamanic cultures, the shaman journeyed into the three shamanic worlds to find wisdom about the spiritual nature of the

Universe. It was here that they met spirits, monsters, and gods. Some of these spirits and gods are fond of humans and would not mind sitting down for a spell to speak of the creation of the Universe or even more mundane topics with mortals. Today, unless we are fortunate enough to be part of a tribe of indigenous people, we do not have spirit walkers and shamans readily available to make these journeys for us, and it is up to us to do this work on our own. In my personal experience with spirits in the Underworld they love to tell you just enough for you to be interested in the journey; but they do not give away all the secrets. You must discover them for yourself, just as you must discover the deeper meanings of the myths for themselves. And to be honest, some of these secrets are immediately useful for you on your path, but others are so mysterious that you may not understand the meaning for days, weeks, or even years.

There are many myths and stories about the Underworld. I have found throughout my research and experience that the Underworld has a similar function in almost every part of the world. Here are some themes that are common from culture to culture in the Underworld myths:

- Underworld as the home of the Dead
- Trials and "Hells"
- Underworld as the home of Monsters
- Underworld as the place of oracles and guides
- Underworld as a place of nourishment, rejuvenation, and healing
- Death and Resurrection

It is also interesting to note that the Underworld terrain almost always looks like the terrain of the storyteller. The Underworld is a mythic reflection of the world we live in now. If there are mountains where the storyteller lives, such as in ancient Greece, then the Underworld has mountains. If there are wetlands, then that is the terrain of the Underworld. We will go over these themes in detail later.

Myths can act as a map to the Underworld. The Norse myths gave directions to which Underworld realm a traveler needed to go. They also go on to say what one can expect to find once they arrive. For example, the lore tells us of the river Slid and it's guardians Modgudh and Garm. As we investigate the Egyptian Book of the Dead, more properly called The Book of Going Forth by Day, there are directions, spells, and information for the dead to maneuver the Underworld to get to the House of the Gods in order to complete a quest for spiritual "resurrection." It is likely that ancient shamans were trained how to leave their bodies. This is now referred to as "astral projection" or "shamanic journeying". It was recommended that they "practice" the Underworld journey often because part of their healing was to perform soul retrievals for the community. This entailed journeying down into the Underworld to find an aspect of a person's soul or consciousness so that they could return it to the person for them to find health and wellness. Sometimes, when someone died, their spirit may have been confused or did not realize they had transitioned into death. The shaman would escort the spirit into the Underworld and the land of the dead as a psychopomp.

Learning about the myths and journeying in the Underworld is a special kind of magick. It was never thought of as a place to be feared, but as a reservoir of power to be used for healing. Most often the rites and rituals of the Underworld were kept secret. The priests and shamans of the ancient world believed that the common person would not be able to understand the mysteries of the Underworld. These sacred mysteries were kept hidden until a seeker who appeared ready for the dark journey made– themself known to them. Only then could true transformation take place. The priests believed that those who were not ready for the mysteries would surely profane them. This is why the Eleusinian Mysteries, a tradition in ancient Greece which celebrated the mysteries of life and death, were kept secret. Those who broke the secrecy were punished with death.

To take the Underworld journey is to become a more spiritual and evolved being. One of the most common ways to do this is to take what Joseph Campbell called the "The Hero's Journey." By taking a journey or adventure into unfamiliar lands, the soul and spirit of the hero becomes transformed into something greater. In myth, the hero would often go on a quest in search of some great thing. The thing could be anything from a treasure to a concept or power. Along the way, the hero would have many adventures, battles, and near-death misses. The hero would also meet fantastic creatures and lovely beings. At the end of the adventure, the hero would understand, through experience, the order of the cosmos and more importantly, who he REALLY is. This self-discovery could not happen if the hero did not take this adventure. It could only be accomplished because of the odd and fantastic things that occurred. This is the very task that you will be undertaking.

On a personal level, learning, mapping, and navigating the Underworld helps us learn about our own subconscious in all of its complexities. On a macrocosmic level, we are traveling through the soul of the Universe. Exploring the Underworld realms allows us to go on a journey of self-discovery. We will be challenged and tested. We are tested in the Underworld, not to show the gods and spirits how good or powerful we are, but rather to prove to ourselves what we are made of. The Underworld journey will show us our strengths and at the same time show us our greatest fears. We are not meant to "pass" every test and gain rewards. There will be many times when we fail. We may try to perform a task over and over again and fail each time. But it is through these mistakes that our soul will learn, grow, and transform into something that is greater than it was before we started the quest. The travels that we have ahead of us are not meant to be simply landmarks that we can say we "have been there"—they are places of great power. It is the kind of power that allows us to spiritually evolve. There is a magical quest ahead of us. There will be many trials, many triumphs, and many strange and mysterious discoveries. Through all of this, we will learn more about the Universe and the deeper meaning of our own spirit.

1
Underworld

The concept of the Underworld may be unfamiliar to some people who have not had shamanistic training or experience. Let us discover what the Underworld is and how it relates to us here in the physical plane. In several cosmologies, the world we live in is the here and now; this is our foundation or the Midworld. The world of the gods and other beings is the heavens or Upperworld. But there is a world that is "under" our own. It is a world that few understand and even fewer have visited. People who come from a Judeo-Christian background call this world Hell. The idea of Hell got its origin from one of the Nordic Underworlds called Hel or Helheim. This is a pagan Nordic world of the Ancestors. In Christian belief any world that was of pagan origin had to be a world of the Devil. A brief overview of pagan myth and legend tells us that the Nordic Underworld has its rough terrain, but it is not a place of despair and torment. Instead, the Underworld is a necessary part of the cosmos and the spiritual nature of the Universe. Without it, there would be no order to the Universe. The Nordic Underworld has many inhabitants; some of whom are the Ancestors. Helheim is the home of the Ancestors that is governed by the Goddess of Death, Hela or Hel. It is her duty to keep the Ancestors safe and she does not allow her inhabitants to leave except under special circumstances. Without Helheim, the dead would roam freely upon the Midworld and cause destruction and havoc. In some cosmologies, allowing the dead to walk the land of the living may bring disease or death. This is perhaps because the dead may have had the energies of death around them that may affect the living.

In many myths, the Underworld is the place where the spirits of the dead dwell when their lives in this world have ended. It is most often described as a place of peace and rejuvenation where the spirits of the dead are kept happy and safe. In other myths, the Underworld has many other terrains that are both mysterious and frightening. But in both belief systems there is great power. There are stories of gods and heroes who adventure down into the lower depths of the universe, who seek treasures, healing, power, and even the return of the dead to the land of the living. But, as in all aspects of creation, there is an order that must be maintained, otherwise chaos would wreak havoc throughout the three worlds. In the vastness of the Underworld, powerful spirits dwell—guardians and gods who protect the powers under our world. There are spirits that guard places of wisdom. It is also believed in some cosmologies that the Fates live here and to spy upon their work is to know one's fate. There are also very ancient deities that harbor the powers of mass destruction. There are tales of great magick and powerful allies who reside in the Underworld. These powers and entities can help us on our evolutionary path; or, if used unwisely, could lead to the very destruction of the known universe.

The Underworld is expressed in symbols and metaphor. In pagan cosmology, the Universe is often portrayed as held together by a Great Tree. In Nordic myth, this Great Tree is called Yggdrassil. Imagine a gigantic tree with a trunk so large you cannot see the end; branches so tall they go into the deep reaches of space; roots that go down into the furthest reaches of the Earth. Some believe that this tree exists in the astral realm, which I will talk about shortly. The trunk represents all that is in the Midworld or the physical existence that we live in. This includes all living humans, animals, nature, and the cycles of our Earth. The great branches represent the Upperworld. This includes the gods, angels, planetary intelligences, star peoples, and spirit guides. The great roots represent the Underworld itself. This is a place of the Ancestors, gods of death, and many other beings that we will learn about as we go further in our discoveries.

The Psychological Underworld and the Mind

Ever since the idea of shamanism was introduced to modern society, people have asked the question, "Are the three worlds real or a part of the imagination?" I think this is a very valid question. Are we really journeying for healing or are we simply deluding ourselves? To answer this question, we should look at the indigenous cultures that put shamanic techniques into practice. There are many instances where the person has been healed with soul retrievals and other shamanistic practices. How does this work? Is it a placebo effect or is it actual spirits coming to heal the person in question? I believe both answers are true. One way to view this is to understand that the human mind acts as a vehicle for traveling into other worlds of reality. Another way is to think of the mind as a mirror of what is happening in the three worlds, much like a television monitor projecting to your living room what is happening far away. Skeptics may ask, "If it is only the imagination, does shamanism still have the capacity to heal me?" Yes. It does. It does because if we try to understand our mind psychologically, we will find that our mind has the wonderful ability to heal itself, the body, emotions, and our spirit. Some psychotherapists are using shamanic techniques to help heal their clients. In her book *Shamanism and Spirituality in Therapeutic Practice*, Christa Mackinnon uses shamanic journeying to aide her clients in healing. In her book she states that shamans, "work towards integrating the different aspects of the mind with each other and with the body, as well as the mind/body with the soul and spirit, and furthermore the individual with the wider community and the community with 'the whole and the spirit'."

To heal and make transformations within ourselves, there must be communication between the subconscious and the conscious mind. Our subconscious thinks in emotions, symbols, and imagery. It is also the seat of repressed memories, desires, fears, and our shadow self. The Shadow Self holds our emotions and memories that we have repressed within our subconscious. It is also the primal, animal self that we may feel has no place in our modern "civilized" society. It does not think in the logical state that our conscious mind does. This is one of the reasons that dreams are often wondrous and strange. Imagery and symbols, such as those found in the Underworld, have a powerful effect on the subconscious. By using imagery and symbols, the subconscious begins to open itself up more and delivers information to our conscious mind. When we journey to the Underworld, we can say that we are visiting some aspects of our subconscious mind. There, we may meet strange beasts, friends and family long dead, and men and women of great power and wisdom. They are all symbols. We may also discover archetypes. In her book, *Journeying: Where Shamanism and Psychology Meet*, Dr. Jeannette M. Gagan says, "…the spirit world encountered in journeying is none other than the landscape of this collective unconscious illuminated by the release of archetypical energy long bound to its internal matrix."

As we journey into the parts of the Underworld that are dark and mysterious, we will most likely come across the Shadow Self. The Shadow Self is the part of the consciousness that holds our repressed fears, secret desires, and prejudices. The Shadow Self is only interested in self-preservation. It has no need for spiritual evolution because this would destroy it. The Shadow Self gets its energy from fear and negative reinforcement, including negative thoughts and feelings we have about ourselves. This is one of the reasons we use the term "personal demons." This phrase is fairly accurate. The Shadow Self is responsible for our uncontrolled anger, deep depression, and the abuse of others. It only serves to harm us in the long run. In the Underworld, we come across our Shadow Self in a number of forms and symbols. Remember, our subconscious speaks to us with symbols and archetypes, so this is how our Shadow Self will manifest. Most often, the archetypes that will appear are monsters, vampires, trolls, and demons. The most common way to deal with these symbols is to destroy them, but it will serve you better if you confront them head on and find out who they are and what they want. Most likely, they will reveal themselves as fears and negative emotions you must deal with. By transforming these shadow archetypes, you can potentially release a lot of the energy that may be blocking your self-healing and transformation.

The subconscious can reveal your own personal monsters, but it can also reveal personal healing and transformation. The Underworld is not just a sewage pot filled with monsters and devils, it is a place of wonder and a place of the Ancestors. There are many beings and spirits there that can aid in your personal healing. They can also take you to places that have the power to heal. The Underworld is filled with many myths and stories about wise women with magick potions and sacred wells and other places that have transformative powers. So how does this relate to the subconscious mind? We all have heard that the mind can aid in our own healing and wellbeing. How do we access this healing at will? We do it by journeying into our mind and finding healing through symbols and archetypes. Indigenous cultures as well as modern holistic healers understand that the deep subconscious holds powerful healing. By journeying to the healing places in the mind's Underworld, we can give our subconscious "permission" to open its healing powers to us.

The question still remains: is the Underworld journey real or is it just in our imagination? Again, it is both. There is an age-old axiom that states, "As above, so below. As within, so without." This is my theory of how it works: your mind is your catalyst to enter the Underworld. It is the vehicle in which you travel. A strong and healthy mind leads to more productive journeys to the Underworld. You must begin to think of it as peeling the layers of an onion. The deeper you are able to journey into your subconscious mind and transform your personal issues, the deeper you will be able to journey into the Underworld and discover new things about the universe and yourself. Also remember that some of the entities that you come across will have strong psychic abilities and will be able to read deep into your subconscious. They may even be able to use your Shadow Self against you. This is one of the many reasons why it is so important to constantly learn about your fears and insecurities. Only through learning about these less than pleasant aspects of ourselves can one transform and evolve. If you are caught off-guard, then your deepest fears can be used against you. Seek to be better than you are. Be brave and go through those things you fear the most. Once you have faced yourself and begun the healing process of the deep mind, you will truly become a powerful, spiritual person. So, what if there is no Underworld and it is all in your head? As longs as you find healing and are transformed, then it does not matter. Healing is healing, no matter if it is found in a magical place far away, or a symbol that reveals your true inner self within your mind. As long as it works...do it!

Creation of the Underworld

Different mythologies explain the creation of the Underworld in many different ways. Several myths claim that the Underworld was created as a sort of cosmic "storage unit" for the Universe. They tell of gods who do not want the dead near their dwellings, as with Greco-Roman cosmology which places the dead far beneath the world in a subterranean world called Hades. Other myths say that the gods of the Underworld who controlled death and the comings and goings of the dead, loved the dead so much that they could not bear to be apart from the spirits. Therefore, the gods and the dead must forever dwell together down below. Many myths often also say that evil monsters, unwanted gods, demons, and strange and unusual creatures live in the Underworld because they are not wanted anywhere else, and the Underworld is open to all who seek its refuge. Some examples of this are the Titans of Greek myth and demons of Judeo-Christian myth. There are also tales of the Underworld being an accident of creation and that the creator gods never intended for it to exist. If we take a look at the Kabbalistic Underworld called the Qliphoth, we will find that it was created when the higher planes, called Sephiroth, were being formed. The Qliphoth is the culmination of the "shells" that were cast off from the creation of the universe.

When you learn more about the Underworld and work with those energies you will discover that the Underworld has a very holy and divine purpose. That is no accident. It is true that there are those Upperworld gods who do not go down to the Underworld and have a disdain for it. That is simply because their energies and powers do not resonate with those of the ancient worlds below and their powers are best suited for the Upper and Midworld. Usually, those gods send messengers down below. If we take a look at the King of the Gods in Greco-Roman lore, Zeus, we see that he will send Hermes, the messenger god, to the Underworld to speak with the Underworld god, Hades. I believe that the Underworld carries a lot of magical power and wisdom. It holds the memories of the past and the visions of the future. By working with these energies one can obtain much personal transformation and growth.

Why go to the Underworld?

We go to the Underworld for several reasons. One of the most common is for personal transformation. The Underworld has places of great wisdom. One such place is the Well of Mimir. Mimir is a Nordic god of wisdom and is often sought out for this purpose. The wise Mimir can tell you many truths and oracles, but sometimes the cost may be great. For Odin, the Norse All-Father, the price was one of his own eyes. Another reason to journey to the Underworld is for prophecy and oracle work. The Underworld is fluid in the sense that it is not as physical and rigid as the Midworld and its laws of time and space are very different from our own. This gives the spirits and entities the advantage of seeing things from the past, present, and future much more clearly than Earthbound humans. The Underworld is also a place of healing and renewal. There are many fountains, springs, and lakes that flow from below the Earth into our physical world. These waterways are sources of great healing. Therefore, the Underworld contains much healing power. One such myth that represents this power is the quest for the Grail. Healing, in most traditions, means to bring someone or someplace back into wholeness. The Underworld is a place of transformation and evolution; therefore, the Lower World has the power to bring much healing to us. One of my favorite reasons for traveling to the Underworld is to connect with the Ancestors. The Ancestors are our direct link to family and our divine purpose in this life. They can help us do many things on the spiritual levels. The Ancestors are our family, and they have a great interest in us that many of the gods and spirits do not. It is amazing how much your personal gnosis and magick grows once you have reconnected with the Ancestors.

We may also travel the Underworld to prepare for our own death. To most people, this seems like a strange and morbid idea. To the ancients, preparing for the moments that led up to and followed the death process was especially important. The Egyptian Book of the Dead and the Tibetan Book of the Dead were created for this reason. Not only were these books written to help the newly dead find their way through the Underworld, but they were also written to help each person mold their consciousness in such a way that they were literally practicing for their death. If you think about it, it makes more sense to practice going through the Underworld so that you may battle demons, meet your Ancestors, and join with the gods. The theory was that if you fail this task, you could become lost or trapped in the Underworld. I think of it like rehearsing for a play or a show. The more you practice, the better prepared you will be.

Odin's Sacrifice (Norse)

All-Father gazed into the cosmos. He saw all of Creation. He saw Yggdrasil, The World Tree. The splendor of the universe spun around its axis point. Odin, who constructed the earth with his brothers out of the corpse of the giant Ymir, looked upon his work in wonder. It took on a life of its own. He knew the cosmos was perfect the way it was. There were many mysteries—many things to discover. Everything was given the power to create life on its own. The cosmos gave off nine magnificent lights. Even the dark worlds had their own magnificent light. These lights were a mystery yet to be discovered.

Later, Odin felt the bliss of the Great Tree, Yggdrasil. He could feel the pulse of life streaming from the Universe into his body. The pulses began to grow more powerful. They penetrated his body with such energy and beauty that he became overwhelmed with ecstasy. He could hear the chorus of songs coming from deep within Yggdrasil. Such beauty. Such bliss. He stretched out his arms and fell. Further and further, he fell into the tree. No horse carried him. No chariot drove him. No spirits accompanied him. He fell into the greatness of creation. He was a comet that fell into the blackness of the tree. Suddenly, he was pulled up short and stopped, so that he was swinging on the branches of creation. "What is keeping me here?" he thought. "Is it a rope? Or is it some other magnificent power that is holding me in this blissful place?"

His mighty spear was in his hand. He had carried it all the way down with. With a great thrust he stabbed it into his side. His bliss now carried the added ecstasy of pain. Sacrifice, he thought. I must give up my old self, my old way of being. Death is necessary to destroy the old self so that my inner being, that which is closest to the deepest insight of the universe, can be realized. His blood spilt above him like a fountain trying to reach the heavens. "No," Odin, thought, "I am hanging upside down. The blood is spilling down. Or perhaps it is spilling up. No matter. Where I am, I am." Odin seemed to float endlessly on the tree of creation. All things seemed to stop in place. If he looked in other directions, he could make out one of the nine worlds. "No, my mind is leaving me! There is nothing down here. Wait, is that life I see?" The mighty Ash rotated in such perfection around him. The energies coming to him from the tree were powerful. But they were not just energies. They were magnificent voices, singing the praises of the cosmos. Days passed; each one more agonizing and blissful than the last. It was not the bliss of pleasure, but rather the bliss of sacrifice. Pain and pleasure mingled into one. More days passed. Odin was one with the tree. He was cradled with beautiful voices streaming to him from the tree. For a moment he wondered who the voices belonged to, but his consciousness faded. Nine days in all was his sacrifice.

There was a glimmer above him. A magnificent power. A magnificent voice, no, many voices singing to him the praises of the universe. They sang songs of prosperity, love, death, and magick. Odin regained his consciousness. The voices streamed with such energy that they wrapped a brilliant light around him: a cradle of magick and power. He looked above his head to see the magnificent lights spinning round, singing the songs of magick, power, love, and death. Such sweet, beautiful glyphs; so simple and complex at the same time. He saw a drop of his own blood fall into the waters of the Underworld. The alchemy of blood and water took the form of another mystery, a Rune. The runes spun around him with the splendor of the universe. They entered Odin's body, entered his mind, and his spirit. Much power poured through his veins. This was Magick. Odin took the runes back to the nine worlds where they would always sing the spells of creation, destruction, and rebirth.

The above myth is my interpretation of Odin's sacrifice to the Runes. Odin journeyed down into the Underworld to obtain wisdom and power. This wisdom manifested as the Runes that the Nordics use for divination and magick. Myths were never meant to be stagnant or dogma. Myths can be seen in the spirit worlds as living and evolving stories that teach mankind in way that we can best understand in our current times. I will admit that this style of the myth appeals to my imagination.

Mapping the Underworld

The Underworld has many wonders and spectacles to see. It is vastly different from what we are used to here in the physical world. At times, when we think it looks familiar to our world, we quickly learn that things are not what they seem. Children's stories are full of wells that lead to magical places or a ferry boat that leads us into a distant land in the west. Stories of the Underworld tell tales about beautiful landscapes as well as the most mysterious places ever discovered. These stories have warnings embedded in them that we would do well to heed. In *Alice in Wonderland* by Lewis Carol, we see how Alice falls into a hole in the earth and is transported into the Underworld. Once there, she sees many wondrous things including smiling cats and a Queen of Hearts.

We must always remember that the Underworld is technically the Spirit world. The rules and laws there are different from our own, but they are still laws. In our world, the laws of physics are solid and firm. We know that the sun comes up in the morning in the East and goes down at night in the West. We know that mountains are solid, and the oceans are cold and wet. We know that winters are cold, and summers are hot. We know that life is both powerful and fragile. We know that there are twenty-four hours in a day. The Underworld is quite different. There are many illusions and things are not always what they seem. This is not a trick intended to confuse travelers or the dead. There is a purpose for everything. Illusions are put in place to keep out those who do not belong in certain parts of the Underworld. It keeps beginners from stumbling upon things that can really hurt them physically, mentally, spiritually, and emotionally. Sometimes the illusions that we discover come right from the minds of the traveler. The Tibetan Book of the Dead has many prayers to the newly dead, or the person preparing for death, that remind them of their purpose in the Underworld and that many of the fantastic creatures, gods, and monsters are a part of their own deep-rooted desires manifesting in the world of spirit. At other times, illusions are there to test the traveler. The deeper one journeys into the Underworld, the more complex the world is and the more dangerous are its inhabitants. If you can pass through the illusions as well as your own fears, then you will be admitted into the deeper realms.

Some examples of the illusions you may encounter are monsters that seem to attack from nowhere, fog that goes on forever, cliffs with no bridges or any other way to get across, or oceans with no boats. If you cannot seem to get through the illusion, it is best to believe that the spirits there know what is best; and sometimes it is best to "not wake the sleeping dragon!" Try to find another way. If you cannot, then graciously end your journey and try again a different day. The mysteries of the Underworld are meant to be discovered by those who can bring the wisdom back to the Midworld for the betterment of not only themselves, but all humanity. It is far better to have the intentions of self-transformation and helping your community evolve when going on such a journey than just doing it for sport.

Time and Space

Time does not run the same in the Underworld as it does here in the physical world. There is a sense of time, but it is drastically different from what we are used to. We are so accustomed to minutes, hours, days, and months that it has become routine for us. We can usually tell when a couple of minutes or hours have passed. We can look at the sun and evaluate the approximate time of day from its position. We even have something referred to as a "biological clock". Our bodies have become so used to our perceived time that we often automatically know when to wake up, eat, and go to sleep. As human beings, we are acclimated to the environment around us.

When we journey to the Underworld, time runs on its own terms. Time may run very quickly or sometimes very slowly. There are many myths and stories about people finding themselves in the three worlds and having marvelous adventures that last days and weeks only to return and discover that only a few minutes have passed. There are also the stories of people who have traveled to the Underworld for what they thought was a short time, and upon returning discover that so much time has passed that their friends and loved ones have been long dead. In the story of *Rip Van Winkle*, by Washington Irving, Rip fallows a Dutch man to a hollow hill where they get drunk on beer. When he awakes, he finds his wife and friends are gone and he has been away for 20 years. Part of the reason this happens is because we are so used to our "Earthly" time that our minds and bodies cannot help but try to place the same rules of time we are accustomed to onto the Underworld. The spirits know this and sometimes use it against us, especially trickster spirits and spirits who do not wish to be bothered.

There are many theories about how time works in the Underworld. One theory says that energy and events begin with the source of all things: God, the creator, or the Great Mystery. The energy from the source of creation in the Upperworld then passes through the Underworld, and then to us here in the Middleworld. If we use the Great Tree of Life as a symbol of the connection between the Three Worlds in the Universe this view makes a little more sense. I like to use the analogy of rainfall when explaining this concept. Imagine rain as a symbol of time/events and energy. Rain comes from the sky (Upperworld) then touches the ground going into the roots of the tree (Underworld) and the roots then pull up the rainwater into the trunk of the tree (Midworld). Another theory says that the Energy begins in the Upperworld (future) travels down to the Midworld (present) and then into the Underworld (past). So, which view is right? I think both are. It all depends on your point of view. There are many places in the

Underworld were you can perceive the passing of time and watch upcoming events pass before your eyes. To be able to do this, a few things need to happen. First, you must be able to find these locations. Second, you must appease the guardian spirits that guard these sacred places. Once you can find the places you must have "access" or have the ability to see in the astral (psychic vision) to be able to see the upcoming or past events.

When you are divining from this world with the tarot, runes, ogham, bones, or other such tools, you are accessing these secret realms in the Underworld. The difference is that you are using the divination tools as a medium for the information versus going into the other realm. It may seem less difficult to simply use a divination tool, but you are seeing events with the symbols via the tool rather than seeing things right from the source.

Sometimes, when there is an important event occurring or about to occur, it is better to go to the Underworld and see exactly what is coming. That way, what you perceive can be a lot clearer. Fate and destiny are not set in stone. By using the Underworld to foresee what is coming, we may be able to avoid oncoming negative events or perhaps give power to positive things coming our way.

Entrances into the Underworld

The Underworld seems to be a place that is far away in the world of stories, dream, and fantasy. But we do have the ability to access the Underworld. It is not as hard as you think. There are many entrances that will take us down into the depths of the Underworld. Before you begin your journey, you must first work to suspend any disbelief. What I mean by this is that you just must "go with it." Let yourself believe it is true, at least for now. Allow your mind to become more and more convinced of the reality of the Underworld as you journey and learn about this wonderful place. The second thing you must do is not have too much expectation. Allow the events to unfold before you. You may not see a lot at first, but have gratitude for what you do see and experience and know that you will discover more as you develop experience in journeying. You also must remember that physical entrances to the Underworld are only possible if you journey in spirit form or by astral travel. If you close your eyes and simply jump into a faery mound, do not be surprised if you get a big bump on your head! There are techniques and basic guidelines that need to be followed, especially by the beginner. I will lay these out for you shortly.

To enter the Underworld, you can do several things. You can do a meditative journey to where you send your astral body to a central point such as a Great Tree or stone. This is where I recommend beginners to go first. Using the imagery of a central Great Tree helps balance and orient you to the new sensations of the three worlds. It also usually leads you to more easily accessible realms. Why a tree? Well, the Great Tree is used by many neo-shamans and neo-pagans. It is something that a lot of us agree upon because of its rich history and lore in traveling into the other worlds. It is mentioned in the Nordic sagas as Yggdrasil, the Great Tree that Odin traveled up and down upon into the nine worlds from Asgard in the Upperworld. Some indigenous tribes use a large stone. The stone serves the same purpose as the tree. The middle of the stone represents this world, the top is the Upperworld, and the base is the Underworld. Try both and see which works better for you.

There is also the Celtic cosmology of Land, Sea, and Sky. This is not exactly the same as the four elements of Earth, Air, Fire, and Water. By the time of the Iron Age, most of the ancient Celts lived on the islands known today as Britain and Ireland. Their homeland is surrounded by water. They were very well trained in seafaring and the energies of the oceans. To them, the Land is the Midworld; it is the land of trees, mountains, and rock. The Sky is the land of the gods. The Sea is the land of the Ancestors and subterranean beings. This cosmology may work for you as well, but unlike the Great Tree cosmology it may not bring you to the center of the Universe. In that case it is better to find spirit allies who are willing and able to help you navigate your way from this starting point here in this world.

Once you are used to traveling into the Underworld you may use "hot spots" or Underworld entrances as told in the lore and myth, such as the well that takes the little girl to the realm of Frau Holle in *Grimm's Fairy Tales*. There are many stories and legends beyond ancient mythology that tell of holes in the Earth that lead to the Underworld, such as *Alice in Wonderland*. In some tales there are actual gates that lead down into the Underworld. In Greece and Rome there were Underworld temples that were built into the Earth that were said to be the actual entrance into Hades. In the story of "Mother Holle" from *Grimm's Fairy Tales*, a young girl falls into a well and finds herself in a new land. There she does chores for Mother Holle and is rewarded with Gold.

The Planes of Existence

To better understand how our Universe operates it is important to understand about the planes or worlds of existence. As we have learned, the universe can be categorized as having three major worlds: the Upper, Middle, and Underworld respectively. For the beginner, this is a wonderful place to start, but as you progress in your understanding and experiences of the three worlds, you will find that they overlap and may discover other worlds within those worlds. As an example, the Nordic cosmos has three major worlds, but each world is separated into three more worlds giving nine worlds in all. To further understand the nature of the universe, it is helpful to realize that the Midworld can exist in several modalities or realms of existence. These are the physical, etheric, astral, mental, and spiritual planes. In my experience, the Midworld is the only one to have all of them, including the physical plane. I have found that the Upper and Underworlds only have the astral, mental, and spiritual planes. However, it is interesting to note that the ancients believed the Upper and Underworlds to have an actual physical existence as well. For example, in Greece, the Upperworld of the gods can be found on Mount Olympus and the Underworld could be accessed through rocky underground caves and rivers. For our purposes in this book, we will work with the idea that the only world that has the physical and etheric plane is the Midworld.

Physical

This is the plane, or world, we are most familiar with. It is the physical manifestation of all the other worlds combined. It is what most people refer to as reality. It must be said that reality is a perception. Most Native Americans and Australian Aborigines believe that the spirit/dream world is just as, if not more, "real" than the Physical world. The Buddhists would say that the physical world was an illusion, or maya. The physical world is made up of solids, liquids, energy, and gases. From our human point of view, it is the most tangible. It follows the laws of physics. Its element is Earth.

Etheric

This plane is very closely related to the Physical world. It is an intermediary between the Physical world and the Astral world. Chakras, meridians, and auras of the body are closely related to the etheric world. However, these things can also manifest on the Astral, Mental, and Spiritual planes. One could also say that life force or chi is also etheric. This is the energy that gives the Physical plane (as well as our bodies life). It takes only a little psychic perception to be able to see the Etheric world. Usually, dim lights and an open mind will do the trick. To the person with sensitive touch, the Etheric world feels like "energized fog" or even like going through a spider web. Its element is also Earth.

Astral

This is the plane that is between the etheric and mental planes. It does not follow the same laws of the physical or etheric realms. It exists partly as an intermediary between the Spiritual and Physical/Etheric planes. All life and all things have an astral counterpart. This plane is called "astral" because astronomical phenomenon such as the sun, moon, planets, and stars have an influence on it. It is shaped by our hopes, desires, dreams, fears, and emotions. It is thought that before something manifests on the physical plane, it must first be imagined on the Astral plane. What we imagine briefly appears in the astral plane. When we add energy to our "thought forms," as it were, then they will manifest in the physical plane. This is also commonly thought of as the dream world. However, some believe that the dream world is a separate plane of existence all its own. Its element is Water

Mental

The Mental plane is more abstract than the previous or "lower" planes. It is the plane of logic and thought. It lies between the Astral and Spiritual worlds. When we imagine something or hear the running monologue in our heads, it is happening on the Mental plane. I think of the Mental plane of existence as being the source of all logic and mathematics in the Universe. Everything from atoms to the sum total of the Universe has a mathematical logic to it. Without this the Universe would only be a place of chaos without order. The Mental plane keeps things in a "logical" place of being. However, just because something seems chaotic it does not mean it does not have a divine logical purpose, as we shall see once we delve further into the mysteries of the Underworld. Its element is Air.

Spiritual

The Spiritual plane is the most abstract of all the planes and is often thought of as a plane of pure light. It is the highest of the planes and it is here that all of creation first begins. This is the first created plane of existence by the Source of All Things, The Creator, or sometimes called Great Mystery. There can be nothing in our modern interpretation of existence without the Spiritual plane. It is the place of the gods, angels, and higher spirits, but they can manifest on all planes! It is the plane that is most "refined". This is where our own spirit dwells. Its element is Fire.

Astral Projection and Shamanic Journeying

To travel into the Underworld, you will be using our astral body. The astral body is our energetic double and is sometimes called our body of light. The astral body can be easily controlled by the emotions and the mind. When you become proficient at leaving your body, which is called astral projection, you will have the ability to journey through time and space. You will be able to travel at the speed of thought to anywhere in the Universe.

    I have studied a lot of books and been to workshops that teach astral projection. When I was a novice magician, I remember learning the formulas and magical conjurations that would allow me to leave the body in spirit. The magical spells seemed exceptionally long and the techniques for leaving the body were tedious and it took months of meditation and visualization exercises to even get one's feet wet. To most students, this was daunting and left people feeling more frustrated than empowered. After having received a formal magical training, followed up with a lot of experience traveling to the three shamanic worlds, I can tell you that you that astral projection is very simple; you just have to practice at it with some regularly and not get discouraged if you do not immediately get results. I will give you a couple of fun exercises to do that will get you started. The key here is to visualize as clearly as possible and FEEL the sensations of walking around, seeing, hearing, smelling, and touching. To do this, you simply use your imagination. Visualize. The other key to controlling your astral body is to use logic, imagination, desire, and will. Meaning, you must imagine yourself in the Otherworlds as clearly as possible using logic, then with the desire to travel, you simply will yourself to do so.

The first few times you may wonder if astral projection is just "all in your head." Well, to some extent it is, but it is supposed to be. Remember, the Astral and Spiritual realms are the places of imagination, dreams, and visions. We travel around in the Physical plane in our physical bodies, so we travel around in the Astral/Spiritual with our astral (imagined/visualized) bodies. I know some magicians who will argue with me that I am oversimplifying ancient magick. And I am. If at first it feels like it is "all in your head" go with it. Eventually, you will meet entities, spirits, and gods who will take you to wonderful places and tell you secret information that you simply cannot "make up." The trick here is to have fun and explore. See what you find. Read some of the mythology listed in Suggestions for Further Reading at the end of this chapter and try your best to understand the spiritual meaning behind the stories. Then go have a spiritual adventure.

So, what is all this talk about shamanic journeying? Basically, shamanic journeying and astral projection are the same thing. You are using your astral or energy body to leave your physical body to travel in the spiritual realms of the Universe. The term "astral projection" is more popular in ceremonial magical and New Age communities while "shamanic journeying" is a term more popular in neo-shamanism. At the end of the day, it really does not matter what term you use because the end result will be the same.

Astral Exercise 1

1. It may be helpful to play a shamanic drumming recording. If you have someone to drum for you, all the better. The drumming should be light but audible enough to hear comfortably. If you are using a drum or having someone drum for you, have them beat at a moderately quick pace. If for some reason you cannot get a recording of shamanic drumming, don't worry. It is not necessary to have a shamanic drum beat to astral project. If you do not like shamanic drumming feel free to use any type of music that puts you in a trance and makes you feel magical. I will often use synthesized songs that sound ethereal to accomplish this for myself.
2. Sit or lie in a comfortable position. Make sure your back is as straight as possible.
3. Close your eyes and take a few deep breaths.
4. Relax your body as best you can. Begin with your feet. Tell them to relax and release all tension. Then move up to your calves. Tell them to relax and release all tension. Go up to the thigh, glutes,

back, belly, chest, shoulders, arms, hands, neck, and head in turn, telling them all to relax and release all stress and tension.
5. Imagine yourself getting up and walking around. Remember, this is done entirely with your imagination. Try not to move your physical body at all.
6. Walk around the room you are in and look at the furniture, walls, shelves. Look at yourself. See yourself lying (or sitting) down.
7. When you are ready, see yourself walk over to your physical body and sit or lie back into yourself. When you are close to your body this will most often happen automatically.

Astral Exercise 2

1. Play your shamanic drumming recording or other music as per the previous exercise.
2. Sit or lie in a comfortable position. Make sure your back is as straight as possible.
3. Close your eyes and take a few deep breaths.
4. Relax your body as best you can. Begin with your feet. Tell them to relax and release all tension. Then move up to your calves. Tell them to relax and release all tension. Go up to the thigh, glutes, back, belly, chest, shoulders, arms, hands, neck, and head in turn, telling them all to relax and release all stress and tension.
5. Imagine yourself getting up and walking around. Remember, this is done entirely with your imagination. Try not to move your physical body at all.
6. At this point, see a door or gateway in front of you. Know that the door leads to the World Tree.
7. Step through the door and on the other side see the World Tree. The Word Tree is the largest tree you have ever seen. Its trunk

extends out further than the eye can see going both left and right. The branches go up into the heavens and you cannot see the top of the tree. You can see that the roots go deep into the Earth.

8. This is the Center of the Midworld, and it is your starting point. Until you are very proficient with traveling, you may want to start here.
9. You notice that there is a door in the trunk of the tree leading down, deep into the roots of the tree. Go through the door. You may see a staircase or simply a tunnel.

   Note: You may also simply see a hole in the ground leading down into the Earth, following the roots, leading down into tunnels.
10. Go down further and further into the roots through the tunnel or staircase. Know that you can travel down very fast and sometimes in just a blink of an eye.
11. Finally, when you arrive at the Underworld, take note of the first thing you see? Explore the immediate environments carefully. When you are ready, go back the way you came and back up the tunnels into the World Tree, then back to the Trunk of the Tree and into the Middle World.

Astral Exercise 3

1. Play your shamanic drumming recording or other music per the previous exercises.
2. Sit or lie in a comfortable position. Make sure your back is as straight as possible.
3. Close your eyes and take a few deep breaths.
4. Relax your body as best you can. Begin with your feet. Tell them to relax and release all tension. Then move up to your calves. Tell them to relax and release all tension. Go up to the thigh, glutes,

back, belly, chest, shoulders, arms, hands, neck, and head in turn, telling them all to relax and release all stress and tension.
5. Visualize a spiral of light, beginning at your feet, spiraling around you, going clockwise; it surrounds your entire body. The only thing you can see is the spiral of light. Know that this magical spiral of light is transporting you to the World Tree.
6. This is the Center of the Midworld, your starting point. Until you are very proficient with traveling, you always want to start here.
7. You notice that there is a door in the trunk of the tree leading down deep into the roots of the tree. Go through the door. You may see a staircase or simply a tunnel.

    Note: You may also simply see a hole in the ground leading down into the Earth, following the roots, leading down into tunnels.
8. Go down further and further into the roots through the tunnel or staircase. Know that you can travel down very fast and sometimes in just a blink of an eye.
9. Finally, when you arrive at the Underworld take note of the first thing you see. Explore your immediate environment carefully. When you are ready, go back the way you came and back up the tunnels into the World Tree then back to the Trunk of the Tree in the Midworld.
10. After awakening from your journey, record your experience in your magical journal and ground yourself back to the physical plane. You may do this by eating something light, drinking water, and/or doing "everyday" things around your home.

At this point in learning about astral travel and journeying through the Underworld, it is not about trying to see how far you go or finding exotic places right away. It is about taking the first steps in learning a new skill.

Just as with any skill, it takes practice. You must remember, the astral body is a direct manifestation of your mind, desires, memories, will, and your imagination. What this means is your astral body will look as you want it to and do what you want it to. Usually, the astral body looks like you do now but in more "idealized" form. Therefore, if you look at your astral body in a mirror, you may look younger, stronger, and healthier.

The astral realm itself takes on the appearance provided by your mind, or the group mind. As we have stated before, if there is a locked gate or a blocked entrance way, most likely your subconscious mind has put it there because either you are not ready to go forward in that direction, or you think you are not ready because of your own personal fears. When this happens, try to find out why you cannot go through, or come back later. Group mind phenomenon happens in the Astral/Underworld when we discover ancient sites such as Hades or Hel and they appear exactly as the ancients described them. This is because of the many people who believe they look a certain way. This massive thought forms echoes through the astral and takes form. The more people who believe something to be true, the stronger it manifests. This is the reason why each type of Underworld in every culture around the world exists. This is also the reason why there is no "one truth".

Exercise:
Finding an Underworld Guide and Spirit Animal

In order to successfully journey into the Underworld, it is important to find your spirit animal and Underworld guide. You will be able to explore the Underworld faster and find treasures and allies much quicker than you would if you traveled alone. Also, the spirit animal can protect you from dangers that you are not ready to face. Your spirit animal can also protect you from spirit attacks in the Underworld. Spirit attacks upon a beginner are extremely rare, and I have often found that the "attackers" are really projections of the traveler's own fears. Put simply, the beginning student is "attacking" themself in the Underworld because of their own fears. In essence, they believe the Underworld is a dangerous place, so they imagine danger at every corner. This is simply not the case. The Underworld does have some dangerous places, but the world of the Ancestors is a place of beauty and spiritual transformation. However, your spirit animal can help you fend off this astral thought form should it occur.

Finding Your Spirit Animal

For this exercise, you will travel to the Midworld to find your Spirit Animal.

1. Choose one of the astral exercises from the section on "How to Use Your Astral Body" above and travel to the World Tree.
2. Once there, make the following statement: "I wish to find my spirit animal". Open your heart chakra and reach out with your energies to your spirit animal. You may not know what kind of animal it is. That's ok. Reach out with your heart and they will respond back to you.
3. Begin walking in whichever direction feels appropriate to you. Keep the goal of finding your spirit animal in mind and try to intuit the direction you should go. The landscape will vary from person to person. You may find yourself traveling into a forest, mountains, valleys, or grass plains. Trust your instincts. For the time being, do not worry if you are "making it up." Visualize your surroundings to the best of your abilities.

4. Keep an eye out for any animals you see. You may see several. Some traditions say that you may see other animals, but you will see your spirit animal four times as your walk along your path. This is a good approach to take.
5. If you do not see any animals at first, keep walking. You should eventually begin to see more and more animals.
6. Once you see your spirit animal four times along your path, walk up to it. Ask it, "Are you my spirit animal? "
7. If the animal seems distant, unfamiliar, or unwilling to speak with you, then this may not be your Spirit Animal. If it is not your spirit animal, keep searching.
8. If the animal is your spirit animal then it will feel like a long-lost friend or relative. Your spirit animal may even feel like a part of you. This is because in reality, your totem IS a part of you.
9. Ask your spirit animal its name and record it in your magical diary or journal upon returning to your physical body.

Once you are fully conscious, visualize your spirit animal in front of you. You may choose to dance with them or simply imagine your spirit animal combining with your aura. To combine the spirit animal with your aura, visualize your animal in front of you. See them walking toward you and energetically combining itself with your aura. Know that you can call upon your spirit animal at any time in any world! I recommend getting an animal fetish - a little statue of clay or stone that represents your animal. If you have the fur, teeth, or a claw of the animal, then all the better. These things are not necessary but do help you connect to them in a deeper way

Finding your Underworld Guide

1. Choose one of the astral exercises and travel to the World Tree.

2. Once there, make the following statement: "I wish to find my Underworld Guide".
3. Call upon your totem spirit animal.
4. In the trunk of the World Tree, visualize a door that leads down into the Underworld. Follow this path down.
5. Follow this path down until you reach the Underworld. What do you see? What does the landscape look like?
6. Keep the intention to find your Underworld Guide in your mind. Begin to explore the Underworld. Ask your totem animal to show you the way.
7. Trust your intuition. Look for people along the way and ask them if they are your Underworld Guide. If not, ask them to point out the direction in which you can find your guide.
8. Once you find an entity who is a likely candidate to become your Underworld Guide, ask if they are willing to help you navigate the Underworld. If the answer is "no," the entity is not your guide, and you should keep looking. If the answer is "yes," ask for their name. Then ask your Guide if there is anything they would like in return. If the request is reasonable and you are able and willing to do it, then by all means do it. If not, graciously explain why you cannot meet the request.
9. Know that you can call upon your Underworld Guide each time you enter the Underworld.
10. Come back to the Midworld the way you came. Then open your eyes and journal about your experiences.

The Underworld is a wonderful place to find transformation of the spirit. It is through the myths that ancient cultures have learned to navigate and find their way through the strange terrain. The power of the Underworld has many great rewards for us and to the community we serve. As we learn how to use our astral bodies, we will begin to further our understanding of the world that holds a vast amount of wonder and beauty. Take some time and discover what the Underworld has in store for you. Journal your experiences and the beings you encounter. Write down what happened and the names of the spirits and gods that you meet. Each day you will develop and strengthen your relationships with the Underworld beings, ancestors, guides, and many other spirits who will help and guide you upon your spiritual path.

2 Navigating the Underworld

The Descent of Ishtar

Ishtar knew all things in Heaven and Earth, but she did not know the secrets of Death or the Underworld below. One day, she decided that she must also know the secrets of the Underworld, so she journeyed to the depths below. When she arrived at the gates of the Underworld, she noticed how gloomy and dusty the place was—like a world that the gods had forgotten. She demanded that the gatekeeper open the gates! She told him that if he did not, she would crash down the gates herself and release the dead so that they would rise to the Midworld and destroy the cosmic order of things. The gatekeeper bade her wait so that he might announce her arrival to Ereshkigal, The Queen of the Underworld, who was also her sister.

When Ereshkigal heard of her sister's arrival, she was very angry. She knew that Ishtar had arrived seeking more power, perhaps even her power! Ishtar was already one of the rulers of Heaven. Would she rule the Underworld, too? Ereshkigal told the gatekeeper not to give her sister special privileges. She would be treated as any other who entered the Realm of the Dead. The gatekeeper went back to Ishtar and allowed her to come through the first gate, but to do so she would have to remove her tiara. When she asked why she must remove her tiara, the gatekeeper relied, "These are the rules of the Queen of the Underworld."

Ishtar approached the second gate, but before she could enter the gatekeeper bade her remove her earrings. When asked why he replied, "These are the rules of the Queen of the Underworld."

Ishtar approached the third gate, but before she could enter, the gatekeeper asked her to remove her necklace. When asked why he replied, "These are the rules of the Queen of the Underworld."

Ishtar approached the fourth gate, but before she could enter, the gatekeeper asked her to remove her garment pin. When asked why he replied, "These are the rules of the Queen of the Underworld."

Ishtar approached the fifth gate, but before she could enter, the gatekeeper asked her to remove her girdle of birthstones from her wrist. When asked why, he replied, "These are the rules of the Queen of the Underworld."

Ishtar approached the sixth gate, but before she could enter, the gatekeeper asked her to remove her bracelets and anklets. When asked why, he replied, "These are the rules of the Queen of the Underworld."

Ishtar approached the seventh and last gate, but before she could enter, the gatekeeper asked her to remove her clothes. When asked why, he replied, "These are the rules of the Queen of the Underworld."

Now naked, Ishtar went deep into the Underworld and greeted her sister, Ereshkigal. Ereshkigal was furious at her sister's arrival. Ishtar was used to being Queen of Heaven and Earth and always sat in the place of Honor. Without courtesy, she sat upon Ereshkigal's throne. This infuriated Ereshkigal so much that she made her servants unleash sixty diseases at Ishtar, killing her. Ishtar, by decree of the cosmic order, was forced down into the depths of the Underworld to dwell among the spirits of the dead. When this occurred, the animals among the Midworld would not breed, men and women would not lust for each other and fall in love, and all love and pleasures stopped in Heaven and Earth.

In the heavens, the gods grieved when Ishtar did not return. The wise Ea created a messenger who was a male prostitute. His name was Asushunamir. He had the powers of both worlds and so he was sent to retrieve Ishtar from the Underworld. The powers of the seven gates could not stop him so he was able to pass right through with no effort. When he found Ereshkigal, she could not resist his charms. She was so pleased by him, she granted him anything in the Underworld he wanted. He demanded Ishtar. Ereshkigal knew that the gods had tricked her with a male whore! She granted his wish, but she cursed him to have a horrible life and to be a whore for men! She told her servants to travel into the realm of the dead to retrieve Ishtar. Ishtar was anointed with the waters of life and she went back through the seven gates.

At the first gate, her clothes were brought back to her.

At the second gate, her anklets and bracelets were returned to her.

At the third gate, her girdle of birthstones was returned to her.

At the fourth gate, her garment pin was returned to her.

At the fifth gate, her necklace was returned to her.

At the sixth gate, her earrings were returned to her.

At the seventh gate, her tiara was returned to her.

When Ishtar emerged into the Midworld, she expected to see her lover Tammuz in mourning, as was the custom at the death of a person's loved ones. But to exact further revenge, Ereshkigal had put a spell on Tammuz so that he would be lusting over female prostitutes when Ishtar found him. This was an outrage to Ishtar. Through Ishtar's journeys, she learned the mysteries of life, death, and resurrection.

Entering The Underworld

The Underworld is a vast and magical place. It has been told of in ancient myths, legends, and stories. It is the setting of epic drama and battles. There are more stories and tales of the Underworld than anyone could possibly write about in one volume. It has many different names and many different terrains and landscapes. In many cultures, however, the Underworld is akin to the world of dreams. It is, therefore, much easier to navigate one's way through the Underworld with stories and imagination than through the waking consciousness of logic. We use stories to teach of the three worlds and magick because stories have a deep connection with the artistic part of our brains and the subconscious. Through stories we can tap into the deeper part of the psyche that helps us discover our magical abilities. The Underworld is often described as a dark and terrible place and yet there are also stories that describe it as the most beautiful place one could ever see in the Universe. Regardless of whether it holds dark terrors or shining wonders, the Underworld is shrouded in mystery and magick.

Once you have entered the Underworld, you may find that it is a wonderful and exciting place. How wonderful and exciting is up to you. Before we go further into the Underworld, I would like to share with you my theories about how the Underworld works on the mind, the subconscious, and the imagination.

The Universe is made up of energy. Everything from light and radio waves to rocks and mountains are made up of energy. The energy of light moves at a much faster rate than the energy of physical matter. Knowing this, it is safe to say that the Upper and Lower worlds are made of energy as well. There is no "physical" matter in these worlds, but our minds still perceive the landscapes and environments we encounter there to be physical. This happens because when we visualize something in our mind, or experience something in a dream, our brain does not distinguish between "real" and "un-real." Scientists have recorded brain waves from subjects that see an actual picture and then visualize the same picture in their minds, and the brain waves read the same. What we picture in our minds or see in dreams is not any less real than what we see physically. In fact, I believe that this scientific evidence makes these things even more real. When we go through guided meditations or visualizations, our minds take the energy that we perceive and give it a picture so that our minds can understand what is happening around us. However, this does not mean that the landscapes we see and the entities or spirits we engage with are simply random patterns of energy. On the contrary, all beings and intelligences are made of energy. Our minds simply give it a form that we can understand so we can communicate with it in a better way. This is the reason that the spirits and gods that someone sees on these journeys often appear to be dressed in the clothing of the culture they came from. If you are from Egypt, the gods and spirits you see will look like the people you are most familiar with. So if this is the case, why do we still see the Greek gods in togas and the Nordic gods dressed as Vikings? Simply put, this is because this is how we think they are going to appear. I believe that if Persephone wants to appear wearing a Chanel gown, then she will!

Our imaginations may sometimes fill in the gaps that our mind is having a hard time perceiving. During your first couple of journeys into the Underworld, you may see what you expect to see. When this happens, give yourself permission to let your mind experience what it wants. Even though you may feel like you are making things up, keep moving forward. I believe this is a safety mechanism that your mind has so that you will not become overwhelmed with the new experiences. Over time, you will become more and more comfortable with your journeys and experiences, and you will begin to see more and more things that you did not see before. This may happen in the physical world as well. How many times have you walked down the same sidewalk or road day after day and looked up and saw something new and said to yourself, "Has that always been there?"

On a psychological note, for argument's sake, let's say that everything you experience on your journeys is simply your imagination and nothing more. Say it is nothing but the by-product of an overactive imagination. Even if this is the case, we must remember that we only use a small portion of our mind's functions and capabilities. If we can go into our own psyches to retrieve useful and profound insight and information, then what does it matter if imagination is involved? I choose to go forward with the thinking that the products of my imagination and dreams are real and that the things I experience in the Underworld are just as "real" as anything I experience going through my everyday consciousness. Scientists say that our dreams are linked to our imagination, but to indigenous tribes such as Native Americans, dreams are more real than our waking "reality". As we will soon discover in this book, dreams are our link to the spirit world of the gods and the dead. Perhaps are imaginations are linked to the spirit world as well. As we continue on, I will let you make your own discoveries in this.

As you go forward in your journeys, remember to react to everything you encounter as real, just as a dream is perceived to be real in your mind when you are in the midst of the experience. This will help you in the long run with your journeys and the information you receive from them. At this point, you may be wondering if the things that you encounter would be able to hurt you and cause you harm. The short answer to this question is YES! We must understand that not everything in the Underworld wants to hurt you, but just like living in the physical world, there are dangerous places and entities (corporeal and non-corporeal) that you should avoid. Later, I will give instructions on basic psychic self-defense. At this point, the best way to go forward is to be polite and gracious with all beings that you encounter. Most of the time, honorable behavior will keep you out of trouble. Most of the spirits I have encountered in the Underworld appreciate politeness. However, if you find that does not work and you feel threatened, simply end the journey, and purify your space with a smoke cleansing or a banishing to purify your working space. You may also call upon your gods and ancestors to protect your space energetically.

We must realize that death can have its beautiful experiences as well as its gruesome ones. Neither one is better than the other. They both have their divine purposes. However, the places of beauty are usually easier to navigate. While journeying, if you find yourself in a place that seems dark and dangerous, ask yourself a couple of questions:

1. Do I need to be here?
2. What is my purpose in navigating through this place?
3. Will I know what to do if I am in danger?
4. Do I know how to get back to where I came from?
5. Am I being respectful and courteous to all beings I meet here?

Remember to be polite and courteous to all beings you meet in any of the worlds. When we are journeying, we are strangers in someone's homeland. You do not have the right to journey everywhere. To be allowed to journey through the world is a privilege and the gods, ancestors, and nature spirits will take that privilege away from you should you abuse it. Be kind. Be honest. Have honor in your words and actions and you will do well in your travels.

Landscapes

The landscapes of the Underworld are as varied as the landscapes in this world, perhaps even more so. A lot of them can be related to our own landscapes but we must remember that the energies and powers of the Underworld have their own laws. What you may think will happen, most likely will not. In many myths and legends, there are stories about the landscapes changing at will. Sometimes this is because there is a glamour protecting an entity or a treasure of some sort. Other times, this is because the spirits who live in this area of the Underworld are testing you to see how you will react and how determined you are to continue on your journey. They may also test you to see how well you know the "laws" of the land. Other times, the spirits are tricksters and think it is great fun to confuse you in any way possible. The land of the Underworld is filled with prairies, valleys, mountains, and hills. The terrain can be smooth or rough. There are many mountains with spirits, trolls, dwarves, dragons, and many other spirits who dwell in them. Most of the stories speak of people who find these mountains to be filled with wondrous caverns that hold many wonderful treasures. But be warned! Any treasure in the Underworld is rarely freely given. There is usually some task or favor to be performed! Whenever a task or favor is asked of you, always make sure this is something you are able and willing to do. Never under any circumstances should you steal something or take anything that is not freely given. You will upset the owner or guardian of the treasure and you can be cursed or haunted by a wide variety of spirits. If you do not know if something is yours to have, then leave it.

Caves, Caverns, and Tunnels

When most people think of the Underworld, they think of a place that is filled with tunnels, caverns, and mysterious caves. Most of the Underworld is not like this at all, but there are places that match this description. Sometimes, the beginning journeyer will use an underground tunnel to get deep into the Underworld. Other times, tunnels will lead you from one of the Underworld "realms" to another. You do not always need to use tunnels, but for some people it helps them travel more easily. You may discover caves that hold hidden treasures, magical items, and spirits and beings that prefer dark places. I will give a word of caution: knowing that there are spirits that prefer dark places, be aware that some of them are friendly and some of them are not. If you are unsure about these places, approach with caution and humility. Do not go barging into unfamiliar places. You may upset the spirit that lives there. This is never something we wish to do. Always be polite and courteous. We sometimes forget that spirits in the Underworld expect the same courtesies and we do. We would never enter someone's home unannounced and expect them to be nice to us. Always treat sprits as you would anyone else or how you would expect to be treated.

Stars, Planets, and Galaxies

The Underworld is sometimes considered the Upperworld in reverse; it is in essence inverted. This is not the same as the reverse of something, such as good being the reverse of evil, but rather a mirror reflection of the Upperworld. Thus, the Underworld can be perceived as having a night sky with stars and moons. It also has what is sometimes referred to as the "Underworld Sun." Some say it is dimmer than the sun in the Midworld, others say it is just as bright. It is interesting to note that scientists believe that when our Solar system was forming, everything was developing out of the debris of a star gone supernova and part of the star energy was caught, forming Earth's gravity, and part of Earth's inner core. I find it fascinating that many myths have a little bit of truth in them.

Fire

In the depths of the Underworld, you may find the Land of Fire. Just as in the depths of the Earth in our physical world we have our fiery mantle and core, so does the Underworld have a realm of fire. Fire in the Underworld may have a frightening effect on those who come from a Judeo-Christian background, bringing up tales and myths of the fiery torment of Hell. In myth and practical experience with Underworld energies, however, I have found that fire establishes magical boundaries and is used for purification and transformation. In a practical sense, when working with the dead in the physical world, fire transforms the body into ash, allowing for the spirit to longer be attached to the physical body. In all three worlds, fire may also represent spirit in a rarefied form.

Water

Water is universally associated with the Underworld. Part of it may be the fact that when you peer into still water you can see your own reflection. Ancient people may have wondered, "Is that me? My ghost? Or is the part of me that is in another world?" This is why water has also been considered a portal or gateway into the Underworld. In many of the landscapes in the Underworld there are numerous rivers, streams, oceans, and lakes. Large bodies of water were always mysterious to the ancients and hold a lot of magical power. Water may also represent the translucent dream state and the subconscious mind. The journey by water is to journey deeper into the Underworld mysteries. The Celts have many myths of the Otherworld journey via water. The Voyage of Bran tells of how Bran sets sell into the West only to be caught in the mysteries in the Otherworld.

In the Underworld itself, water is usually associated with knowledge and magical power. To drink of the water is to gain much power, but it is wise to listen to your spirit animal and guides on such matters. There are rivers in the Underworld that may cause you to forget. You may have to begin your quest all over again and re-learn what you have learned. There are also rivers that are made of acid and may damage your astral body. There is much magick and power in the watery places of the Underworld. It is important to learn as much about them as possible before we journey into situations that may have consequences. Psychologically, water also represents the subconscious and the fear of the unknown.

The Well

Wells go deep into the Earth and contain nourishing water that life very much depends on to thrive. In myth, the Earth has great healing powers. With the combination of water from the Underworld and the healing powers of Earth, the well becomes a place of great power. Wells are also a powerful entrance into the Underworld. From the viewpoint of ancient people, the Underworld was "below" and the well went down into the depths of the Earth where the Underworld was said to be. There are many stories of people falling into wells and landing in a strange world below. In Grimm's "Mother Holle," a young girl falls into a well only to find herself in the Underworld. There she discovers the home of Mother Holle and is instructed to do chores for the old woman. Upon returning to the above world, she is rewarded with gold. After seeing this, her lazy, greedy sister jumps in the well hoping to find gold as well. The sister is lazy and does not perform her chores well. Instead of gold, she is rewarded by being covered in pitch.

In the Underworld, wells have even greater power and wisdom. To drink from these wells usually grants the seeker great magical powers and wisdom. However, there is almost always a guardian who protects the well from those who are either uninvited or not ready for the well's power. In Nordic mythology, the sacred well at one of the roots of the World Tree is called Mimir's Well. The well is guarded by the great god Mimir. He can offer you great wisdom. However, as stated before, there is a price. Odin, the All-Father, went to the Well of Mimir seeking wisdom. It would be granted for the price of one of Odin's eyes. Now, All-Father's eye forever remains in the well seeing the great wisdom it contains.

To understand the well and water more fully, it is helpful to understand the Goddess Mysteries of the Underworld too. In Neopagan mythology, the Goddess is often symbolized by the chalice. The chalice symbolizes the womb and the creation of life. The water inside the chalice/womb is the healing and rejuvenating power of the Goddess herself. To drink of the chalice is to literally drink of the powers of the Goddess. This is where we get the Pagan mysteries of the Holy Grail.

Be warned, to drink from the Underworld can be life-changing indeed. The water from the sacred well can grant blessing, healing, and wisdom, but at times, the guardian may claim the seeker for themselves or as a new resident to the Realm of the Dead. Before drinking from the Underworld, find out what consequences there are for those who dare to drink.

Rivers

Rivers in the Underworld have a variety of purposes. In Greco-Roman myth, there is a river of "Forgetfulness" and a river of "Memory." These rivers are to ease the transition of the dead to their new state of being. They also serve to detach the dead from their formal earthly life. If one were to cling to the Midworld, then they may not find peace in the Realm of the Dead. Rivers also have a protective quality. Because they are usually moving, they sometimes keep undesirable entities away. At times they can have a sinister effect. The deeper you go into the Underworld the more mysteries are contained there. There are protective rivers that are "deadly" that keep unwanted beings away. In the Mayan tradition there is a River of Blood and a River of Pus. In Norse myth, there is a river named Slidh that you must cross to get to the hall of the Death Goddess Hel. Rivers are either seen as energies that go to and from the Underworld or are there to test the traveler. Never step into a river. You never know what you will find.

Charon is the ferryman from the Greco-Roman tradition. Once a spirit of the dead finds themselves at the entrance of Hades, he ferries the spirit over the river to the other side. But he only does this if the spirit's body has been buried properly. This is usually done by burial with two coins, one on each eye; this represents money for the ferryman. Those who have not been buried properly are doomed to roam the outer reaches of the Underworld and the Midworld for a hundred years. Only then will they be ferried across. Charon is very stern. However, he has been known to make exceptions in extraordinary circumstances. In a similar fashion, Modgudh and Garm are the guardians of Hel's hall and only they decide who comes and goes in the land of the dead.

Oceans

Oceans surround the landscapes of the Underworld. They make boundaries around different "lands" and realms of existence. Oceans in the Underworld keep the beings of that realm exactly where they are. It is possible to sail on top of the oceans and swim beneath them, but just as our own oceans are vast and dangerous, these oceans are even more so. There are giant monsters and entities that rarely wish to be disturbed. There's a reason these oceans keep the residents of that land safe where they are. In the "Epic of Gilgamesh", Gilgamesh grieves for his dead friend, Enkidu. He set out on a quest to find the gods of death to restore his friend back to life. By the sea, a maiden named Siduri instructs Gilgamesh to travel the ocean of death to find the ones with the secrets of eternal life.

Oceans are also entrances into the Underworld itself. Many myths speak of the Underworld as being full of water and it takes a boat or ship to get all the way through. In the Celtic tradition, if one sailed west, one would find themselves on the islands of the Otherworld and the lands of the dead. From a historical standpoint, seafaring was very dangerous, and many men died from shipwrecks to find themselves forever in the watery Underworld.

Illusions

When journeying into the Underworld, there are many illusions you may encounter. What this means is that what you perceive can be a trick, a mask, or a façade. The Underworld is full of spirits that look like demons but are really gods, or monsters that take the shape of harmless animals and other creatures. This can become very confusing and frustrating to a new journeyer, sometimes to the extent that the journeyer feels that the Underworld is nothing but a trick of the mind or just a figment of the imagination, or sometimes even a cruel joke of the universe. We must remember that the Underworld is a place of energy and does not follow the same rules as our physical Universe. So, yes, sometimes it is like a dream. But for this reason, the Underworld is all the more powerful. One reason that things are not what they always appear to be is that we are not ready for the teachings and the power of the Underworld. Another reason is that by receiving the information too early, you may not be ready to use its full power, or you may hurt yourself or others. There are beings in the Underworld that are very powerful, and you do not want to encounter them until you are ready. Usually, illusions and gates are put in place so that you encounter only the Otherworlds that you are ready for.

The best thing to do is continue journeying and try not to become frustrated when you encounter the strange illusions. Take comfort in the thought that when you are ready for things, they will be revealed to you. I can tell you from personal experience it is better that way. You do not want unwanted things following you back to your home. Not every entity can nor should be friended, but neither should they be banished. "There are more things in heaven and earth" to quote the immortal bard. In my journeys through the Underworld, I once ventured into territory I was unfamiliar with, and perhaps I traveled further than I should have. I sensed a strange entity nearby. I decided to leave and return to my physical body. Upon waking up the strange entity was in my living room as plain as day! I used my intuition and understood that it meant no harm to me. Because I traveled further than any book had described to me, I had no idea how to send the entity back to the Underworld where it belonged. The strange creature spoke no language that I could speak. It took me the better part of the night to get the entity back to its home. It was with the help of my gods and ancestors that I was able to do so. Luckily, the strange entity was harmless. I was lucky. But what if it was not? That is one of the best lessons I have ever learned about traveling further than needed!

Places of Oracles

There are several ways you can use the Underworld as an oracle. One of the ways is through a practice called Seidr. This is a Nordic shamanic practice of journeying to the Underworld to speak with the gods of the dead or the dead themselves. In this practice, one uses the trance technique of swaying and quaking to induce an altered state. Once this is done, the Seidmadr or Seidkona journeys down into the depths of Hel to visit the realm of the dead. With the permission of Hela, they gain access to a certain member of the dead who possess the power of prophecy. Being that events begin in the Upperworld then go down to the Underworld before manifesting on the Middleworld, the spirits have a firsthand view of what is to come to the Middleworld. The Seidr person could also visit Hela herself and ask for prophecy, although this is something that should not be undertaken by people who are not expertly trained in this art.

Another way to gain access to prophecy would be through the Well of Mimir. As we remember, the head of the wise Mimir is in a well that accesses the Underworld. Mimir has the power to foresee all things to come. It is a very dark and unnerving place and those who are clever and brave enough may ask Mimir his questions. Be warned, he will ask for a heavy price for the wisdom he offers. There are also the Three Norns who are said to know the past, present, and future. These are similar to the Three Fates in Greco-Roman myth but have some differences. The three Norns are named Urdr (That which was), Verdandi (That whish is), and Skuld (That which is becoming). They are three great beings who weave the intricate tapestry of Fate. In this tapestry, the magical thread contains everything that was, that is, and that will be for everything in the Universe, even the fate of the gods. The Norns are not as easy to get information about the future from as you might think, however, so be warned.

You may also observe the coming future of events firsthand. One you become proficient in journeying; you may find places where you may perceive the future. Sometimes you stumble upon these places; but often, gods and spirits will reveal these areas of oracles once you have proven your motives. You cannot fool the gods. If you are acting for the good of your own transformation and the good of your community, the spirits will help you. If not, they will either tell you to turn back or send you on a wild goose chase. There are many stories of Underworld entities setting the journeyer on the wrong track. It is best to remember, before seeking oracles in the Underworld, to give offerings to the spirits and gods that you wish to commune with. Even then, this is no guarantee that they will help you.

Realm of the Dead

One of the more commonly known places of the Underworld is the Realm of the Dead. It is here that those who have died and passed beyond the veil reside. It is not a place of suffering, but rather a place of peace, rest, and community. The Realm of the Dead in the Underworld is not a scary place and is not set aside from the Upperworld or realm of the Gods to punish or to keep the people there separate or segregated. The dead are in a different "land" or "world" from the gods and the living because they were simply possessed of a different energy. The energies of the gods vibrate on a much higher refined divine frequency than the living or the dead. Because of this "higher" vibration pattern of the energies, the gods are said to live in the Upperworld. The dead vibrate on a "lower" vibration, so they dwell in the Underworld. There is no judgment on whether the Underworld is better or worse than the higher worlds. In Greco-Roman mythology, Hades is the ruler of the dead, not out of punishment, but because the Underworld is large and contains many riches that lie beneath the earth. In a spiritual sense, Hades rules the dead because it is cosmically ordained by forces greater than he. Simply put, it was the "right" thing to do. They are simply different, nothing more, nothing less. Being a spirit of the dead does not make one any more or less holy than the gods themselves. In fact, some cultures place more sanctity and importance on the Ancestors than they do on the gods. In China, the Ancestors were worshiped above and before the gods. It was custom to give offerings of incense and prayers to the Ancestors. This was important because the Ancestors would provide good luck and financial fortune for the family. In his book *The Deities are Many*, Jordan Paper says:

"The fortunes of the family are dependent on the well-being of the dead members of the family, and the fortunes of the clan on its larger set of dead. Unless the dead are kept well, they will not have sufficient power to assist the family, and unless the dead are pleased, they may not care to help the family."

In Christianity, the belief is that when someone dies, their soul goes to Heaven so that they may spend eternity sitting next to their concept of God. Christianity is a monotheistic religion, and they believe that there is no other place in the Universe other than Heaven that can you find God. The only other alternative is Hell, a place that is believed to exist "under" all of God's creation. In Neo-paganism, we believe in many gods; so whatever world you choose to go to, there will be a god who rules that place. Many Pagans do not believe in a place of punishment. However, there are pagan philosophers, such as Plato (427-347 BCE), who believed in places where a soul would suffer torment for a period of time if it had been wicked in the Middleworld. This seems to serve the function of purifying the soul before it is ready to ascend to the Middle Realm and live a new life. In his book *The Republic*, Plato tells the "Myth of Er". In the myth, Er dies and sees two great chasms. One going to heaven and the other going into the earth. Those who did good deeds traveled into heaven, but those who did evil deeds when into the earth for penance and purification:

"For every wrong he has done to anyone a man must pay the penalty in turn, ten times for each, that is to say, once for every hundred years, this being reckoned as the span of man's life. He pays, therefore, tenfold retribution for each crime, and so for instance those who have been responsible for many deaths, by betraying state or army, or have cast others into slavery, or had a hand in any other crime must pay tenfold in suffering in each crime."

Similarly, in Tibetan Buddhism, people believe in the purification of souls after death. What this means is that the place of "hell" is more of a place where the illusions, misdoings, and self-deceptions are removed to make the soul ready for either reincarnation or to join the Realm of the Dead permanently. There are many versions of this place. While researching different cultures and spiritual philosophies you can see some similarities in the Land of the Dead from culture to culture. They all seem to have aspects of healing and renewal, as well as dark places of despair. In my research on the dark places of the Land of the Dead, it is rare that the gods place the Ancestors in such places. It is the fears and guilt of the dead that seems to impose self-judgment on each individual person. I believe these dark places were created so that the dead would have a place to purge and cleanse themselves of these dark energies.

Some people may be confused as to why there are so many different versions of the afterlife. If there are so many recordings in different mythologies about the Realm of the Ancestors, does that mean that only one is right and the rest are wrong? Does this mean that they are all wrong? In my experience, the answer to this question is that they are all correct! It is the collective consciousness, or in some cases the collective un-conscious that affects the Underworld realms of the Ancestors. Because many people throughout the ages believe something to be true, then the collective power of their minds have a direct effect on the Underworld. It has already been established that the universe or multi-verse is made of energy. Everything from the most "spiritual" essence to the most physical substance is made of energy. Energy is influenced by our minds. This is how we can do magick and energy work. Energy follows thought. In this way, the places where the dead dwell is influenced by that culture. Of course, there is the theory that says that the gods created these places, and we simply are a product of these creations. But this poses the question, did the gods create man or did man create the gods? I personally believe that it is both. I believe that we influence each other. Our environments also influence us. In our minds we create a place that is both beautiful and scary, depending upon what our culture and environment dictates. In quantum physics, scientists are theorizing about the existence of parallel universes. Most of their theories have come from experiments involving protons that are in one place, disappear (possibly to a different universe all together), and then instantly appear someplace else without a direct path. It is also interesting to note that physicists have discovered that photon particles change and alter simply because we are observing them or on some level we are thinking about that energy. There is also the theory that if black holes in space suck in all forms of light, then it must go somewhere because energy cannot be destroyed, only altered. So where does it go? A parallel universe? All of these are fascinating theories that may help us understand some of the complexities of the Underworld.

The realms of the dead are based on the environments that the residents are used to. If you come from a culture that lives in the desert and has sandstorms for days on end without rain, then most people from your culture will believe that the afterlife looks like this, and that is what the afterlife will be. The same is true for cultures from the mountains or rainforests. However, the lives of ancient people were usually very harsh. The priests of these harsh cultures envisioned an afterlife that was free from hardship and instead filled with blessings and luxuries. In the ancient past, religion and the hope of a better afterlife was big business. For many people, this hope for something better after death was all they had. In turn, this is one of the reasons Hell came into being. If the Christian priests could convince people that if they did not worship as they were instructed, then the promise of an easy and peaceful afterlife would be forfeit. Another reason that the concept of Hell as being a place torture and pain comes from the Greco-Romans in the ideal of Tartarus. Tartarus is a place in the Underworld where the Titans are imprisoned because of their destructive nature. It is also a place where some of the dead who caused great suffering to humanity were kept.

Because of mythology, we sometimes envision the places of the afterlife to look the same as they are described in the ancient stories. Remember that when these stories were told, they were very modern places at the time. They told of landscapes that were similar to what the people knew. They spoke of temples and dwelling places that were like their city structures, but which were more magnificent. The most important thing they spoke of was the reuniting with family and friends that had died before. This was a main selling point of the afterlife.

This poses another question: if this is true and each culture has their own version of the afterlife, do they exist in the same place or separately? This question I believe can be answered in the following manner. As we have been discovering, the Otherworlds, especially the Underworld, do not follow the same laws as the physical universe does. Our minds are used to compartmentalizing everything. This goes in this box and that goes in that box. The easiest way to describe it, based on my own experience, is like the layers of an onion. They all exist at the same place but in different levels of existence or dimensions. And yet, this is still only partially correct. Truthfully, I have not found the Underworld do be so easily sectioned off. Even with its many landscapes and places, understanding of the Underworld is not so easily "cut and dried." Energy always follows the path of least possible resistance. So, I believe that both answers are correct. They are in different places separately and yet are in the exact same place at the exact same time.

Beginning Your Underworld Journey

When you first begin journeying into the Underworld, you will encounter strange and wonderful things. When you become more adept at journeying, if you travel deep enough you will encounter things that are both healing and harmful. For now, you will not have to worry about dangerous entities too much. The spirits you will first encounter are those found closest to our world here in Middle Earth. They are those Underworld entities that usually have had dealings with humans in some way before. Any odd or frightening spirits you find during your first initial travels are not trying to harm you. They want to challenge your worthiness, especially when they can tell that you are a beginner. They know this by looking at your energy signature. During your first journeys you may be filled with a sense of wonder and fear. This is normal and the entities will be able to pick up on your emotions. This is another way they will be able to see that you are new to the Underworld. It is better in shamanic journeys to have a goal or intention when traveling through the Underworld. Some say it is mandatory. There are a couple of reasons for this. First, as with any journey, you want to have direction. You may not know exactly where you are going, but you know that there is a goal. The goal will help focus your mind so your subconscious will be better equipped to help direct you. This will also put out a call to any spirits that are willing to help and guide you on your journey. Many goals are quite simple ones, such as: "to meet my Ancestors," or "to map the Underworld," or "to find healing." All these things are good and purposeful, and, as simple as they are, can lead to profound insights and revelations. I personally travel to the Underworld to work with the Ancestors and seek healing for myself and others.

When you begin, you may only see deep caves and ancient forests with large flora. This is common; however, you are barely at the entrance of the Underworld. I have seen many workshops on the Underworld journey where beginners experience finding two-story tall sunflowers and giant bees. This is nothing unusual. You are definitely in the Underworld, but you have not gone that far. I have found that your hopes and fears influence your experiences, especially in the beginning. It is common to see exactly what you think you are going to see. This may make you ask yourself if you are imagining everything. Yes, you are. And no, you are not. You are doing the work correctly. To me, this is a sort of an astral "safety net". Your mind and spirit need to know that journeying to the Underworld is safe, so your mind interprets its experiences in a very non-threatening way. I think students would be scared off if on their first couple of experiences in the Underworld they found some ancient being with three heads and giant teeth! The funny thing is that most spirits that look menacing are powerful helpers. Even in the Underworld, we should never judge something by how it appears! Things that look frightening or strange are usually our own mental projections of our fears placed upon the energy of a being. If we do not understand something, or do not want to deal with a particular energy, our minds may interpret the entity as looking hostile and threatening. This is not to say that there are not hostile entities in the Underworld. There certainly are, but as I have said before, if we are cautious and treat everyone, we encounter in the Underworld with respect we will generally be all right. In the unlikely event that you do encounter something hostile in your first initial journeys there a few things you could do. First, you could simply leave and end your journey. Afterward, I would purify my working space with cleansing smoke. You could also try speaking with the entity. It is better to understand why the entity is hostile. All situations in the Underworld are opportunities for learning. I would not try to banish or send an energy attack at an entity at this point. Remember, you are in their home. You are the intruder. By entering the Underworld with an open mind and an open heart, you will gain many spirit helpers and have many wonderful adventures.

Where The Dead Live

In myths, the dead are taken to the Underworld to live in spirit. This is a place that is well protected from outsiders and keeps the dead safe within this eternal place of rest. The descriptions of the Land of the Dead vary from culture to culture. As I have said before, we see the Underworld and the land of the dead however we think it will look. In many cosmologies, it is taught that the Underworld is a reflection of the Midworld. So, it is only natural that the Land of the Dead reflects our daily lives here. For our Underworld journeys, the Land of the Dead has many mysteries and spiritual wisdom for us to discover. I encourage you to travel to your ancestral Land of the Dead as well as those of other cultures. For some of us, there is sadness hovering over these places. This sadness is ours and we must understand that this feeling is our own and not of the Ancestors. The Ancestors are in a place of healing and rejuvenation. We can sometimes feel sad that they are there because we miss them. Honor your feelings, but at the same time, try to understand that this is where they need to be. There is a cosmic order to things.

The Spirit Wife (Native American Zuni)

A young man's wife had died and he could not stop grieving for her. He sat by her grave, poured sacred corn pollen on the ground, and painted an eagle plume in red. The spirit of the wife came out of the grave and sat down beside him telling him that she was happy in the Land of the Dead. He did not want to be without her, and he was determined to follow her back. She finally agreed to let him follow her. She explained to him that he could see her spirit at night, but during the day she would be invisible and that to follow her, he must tie the red plume into her hair to see where she was going. He agreed.

During the day, the man could not see his wife, only the red plume floating in the air. He followed the plume by day and rested by night. At night, his spirit wife was beside him. For many days, he followed the plume, and he began to grow very tired. Still, he persisted after her. One day the plume walked over a great canyon, just floating into the air. "Wait!" the man said, but the red plume floated to the other side. So, the man climbed down the canyon's side and crossed it. He then began to climb the other side when he got stuck. He could not go forward or backwards. A little squirrel decided to help him and took a nut from his mouth. He stuck it into the side of the canyon and commanded the nut to grow. Out sprang a tree from the side of the canyon and the man was able to climb up to the other side where the red plume was waiting for him.

The man followed the plume to a large dark lake. The plume went down deep into the waters. This was the place of the dead. He despaired because he knew he could not follow the plume. He sat in his grief. An owl saw that the man was crying and decided to help him. The owl told the man to follow him to a cave in the nearby mountain and he would help him. Once, in the cave, the owl was met by his relatives. The owl took off his owl clothing revealing the spirit of a man. He made a magical medicine bag. The bag was sleep medicine. The owl spirit explained that the medicine would put him to sleep and send him to a faraway place and that when he awoke, he was to go to the anthill to await his wife. The owl spirit warned the man that he must have patience or grief would strike him again.

The owl spirit and his relatives flew down into the lake and into the Land of the Dead. There, they used sleep medicine to make the guardians fall asleep. They then retrieved the spirit of the wife. The man awoke and went to the anthill and found his wife in full flesh. But again, he was warned to be patient. They were told to journey back to the land of their birth. Only there, would the wife be fully alive. But he was warned that if he should touch her before they returned home, she could not stay with him. For four days they journeyed back home. On the forth night, before returning home, the wife fell asleep. The husband could not wait anymore! He reached down to touch her, and she instantly awoke! She faded away into spirit and returned to the Land of the Dead. An owl was in a nearby tree. "I told you to be patient!" he said. The owl explained that is was just as well, because if no one ever journeyed to the Land of the Dead, then the Earth would be too crowded.

Hades/Elysian Fields

Hades is the Land of the Dead in the Greco-Roman pantheon. Hades is named for the Underworld itself and the god Hades that rules there. Hades was originally called "The House of Hades" but was shortened to Hades. The Creator Gods of the Greco-Romans divided the Universe into three parts. The Upperworld ruled by Zeus/Jupiter, the Midworld ruled by Poseidon/Neptune, and The Underworld ruled by Hades/Pluto. In the eyes of the ancients, this division kept the Universe in cosmic balance. Hades had many different landscapes and levels. To get to Hades, a spirit of the dead had to cross the River Styx guided by a dark ferryman named Charon. Once you were taken to the entrance of Hades, your spirit was then met by the three-headed dog, Cerberus. The role of this giant creature was to keep the souls of the dead in and the living out. Once within the gates of Hades, one encountered the dark spirits that caused disease and death. Modern spiritualists would call these entities demons, but the ancient Greco-Romans did not view dark spirits in the same way as we do now. It was at the entrance that these dark spirits waited to be released so that they could cause sickness, harm, and death among the living. As we enter through this part of Hades, these dark spirits may be curious about us, but they will not harm you. If we maintain a healthy lifestyle, we will have a bright healthy aura, and entities cannot "latch" on to us. If we are in a place in our lives that we have bad habits and making poor health choices, then we may have a weekend aura that may cause lower spirits to cling on to us. If you are unsure whether you have a lower spirit clinging on to you, purify yourself with incense or a bath upon your return to the physical plane.

There is a river of Memory and a river of Forgetfulness in Hades. The purpose of these rivers is to make the blessed spirits of the dead forget their troubles and loved ones in the Midworld so that they can remain happy in the fields of the blessed. For those who did wrong in life, they would remember their crimes for all eternity.

There were many paths in Hades that held the sorrows of the dead. At the end of one path were the spirits of those who were killed because of love, either by suicide, scorned lovers, or simply dying of unrequited love. On another path, were the eternal battles of the fallen soldiers. There was also a path for those who committed crimes in life and were not punished. Above these souls, boulders always threatened to crush them so that they would forever be on edge and unhappy. It is easy to see that these torments may have been put here by the souls' own making. In the Underworld, our beliefs, conscious or not, are manifested. This is one of the reasons we see the Underworld the way we think it will look like. If our guilt is overwhelming at the time of death, we will carry this guilt with us, and it may manifest as torments. But this will only happen if you are convinced, upon death, that you need to be punished. To me, this is one of the aspects of karma. You pay for your "sins" because you believe you must. These paths of Hades were a self-imposed punishment of sadness, grief, anger, and guilt. This is also one of the reasons that religions speak of living a good and pure life. In this way you do not put shackles on yourself once you cross over to the Underworld.

There is a place of the blessed people called the Elysian Fields. Priests, poets, lovers, songwriters, and anyone the gods favored spent eternity here. In some myths, the Elysian Fields are in Hades, and in others, the fields are in the far side of the Earth at the edge of the ocean —much like in the Celtic traditions about the Isles of the Dead. The Elysian Fields is a place of happiness, warmth, and bliss, and it has a sun, moon, and stars of its on. When one enters this wonderful place, they can see people dancing and feasting, playing sports, or simply strolling through the magnificent fields. This is a place where one often hears songs and poems being read.

There is a dark place in Hades called Tartarus. When one sees the edge of the cliff that leads down to this horrible place, it is said that it is as deep as Heaven is high above. Tartarus can be somewhat related to the Christian Hell and perhaps this is one of the sources where the Christians originally got the idea. Tartarus is a prison in the Underworld. It is a place where the wretched beasts such as the 50-headed Hydra is kept. It is also where the Titan race of gods is kept bound with divine chains so that they will never again cause chaos and havoc in the Universe.

The rulers of Hades are Hades himself and Persephone, his Queen. It should be noted that in ancient times, one never gave offerings to Hades because the thought was that by doing so you would invite Death into your home. Instead, you would give offerings to the lovely Persephone. It was she who walked among living people for six months out of the year and understood them. Hades was considered too far removed from us and his heart was thought to be cold. However, the beautiful and kind Persephone could melt his heart with only a glance. To give her offerings and win her favor was to win the favor of Hades. It is often said down in Hades that Hades could not deny any request made by his wife.

When I go down into Hades, the first part is usually the same. I astral project myself to the River Styx where I am met by Charon the ferryman. For a token, I am taken across the river to the gates of Hades. Cerberus is used to my comings and goings, so he does not bark or growl at me. He barely notices me and allows through. I'm sure he has more important things to do than worry about a living Spirit Walker going into Hades. Once inside, the caverns are vast and deep. I quickly make my way to the Realm of the Ancestors. The place of the Ancestors, from my experience, is not a place of gloom, but a place of bright colors and everyone is happy for the most part. I often say that the Ancestors are "living" their lives, but in this place, they happen to be dead. The Ancestors here are, of course, Greco-Roman with the occasional outsider who chose upon death to live their afterlife in this magical place. I always ask for an audience with Hades and Persephone when I am there. There are many tales of Hades being dark and brooding, but I rarely see him that way. I see him as a kingly father figure who protects the dead and keeps the Chthonic Gods safely secure. I once asked Hades why he keeps the dead in the Underworld, and he replied with this:

"I do not keep the dead here as prisoner. I keep them safe. The dead are my children as the living are the children of Zeus. Most other gods are too busy or have no need of the dead, but I would never cast them off. They are my people, my children, my friends. I would do anything for them."

Tartarus is also a place I like to visit. Sometimes Hades will escort me. I believe this to be out of protection for me rather than a formality. It makes him sad in some way that his own ancestors are kept locked up in the depths of the Underworld, but he knows the Universe cannot survive with them. Not just yet.

Hel, The Nordic World of the Dead

In Nordic cosmology, there are nine realms or "worlds". The worlds are pictured as rotating around an enormous ash tree, called Yggdrasil. There is a lot of lore on where the nine worlds are, but I take some liberties in their placement based on my own experience with the energies of these fantastic worlds. In the branches of the cosmic tree are the three Upperworlds: Muspelheim (the primal realm of fire), Asgard (realm of the Aesir gods), and Vanaheim (home of the Vanir gods). Rotating around the trunk of the cosmic tree are the three Middleworlds: Ljosalfheim (home of the Light Elves), Midgard (the physical world), and Jotunheim (the home of the Giants). In the roots of the Great Tree are the three Underworlds: Svartalfheim (the realm of the Dwarfs and Dark Elves), Helheim (the home of the Dead), and Niflheim (the primal realm of ice). The world of the dead is called Helheim or sometimes just Hel. The Christians took the Nordic Underworld world of Hel to represent their fiery world of torment that they now call Hell. To the Norse, Hel was not a place of torment at all, but a place for the dead to rejuvenate and rest.

When someone dies, they are sent to the Underworld realm of Hel, unless they die in battle. If a warrior dies in battle, then they are either chosen by Freya, the goddess of love, or Odin, the All-Father, to live in his great hall of Valhalla, the hall of the slain. Most of the Nordic people were not warriors so many went to live with the Goddess of Death, Hel or Hela. Hela is said to be half beautiful maiden and half rotting corpse. The poems and writings never tell which half is which. Some say the left side of her face is rotting while the other half is beautiful. Some say that from her waist up she is a beautiful maiden, but if you were to look under her robes you would see the rotting flesh from her waist down. I see her neither of those ways. When I journey down to the realm of Hel, Hela always appears as a beautiful Goddess of Death. However, as I speak with her, her form flickers back and forth between maiden and rotting corpse. It can be quite disconcerting if you are not prepared for it. I think she thinks it is quite fun to see journeyers in her realm become startled by her rotting corpse form. Hela is a gracious goddess and takes great care of the dead who come to her. She is the Mother Goddess of the Underworld and has vowed that all the spirits of the dead who come to her will be taken care of.

The world of Hel can be dark and dank in places. There are certainly parts of Hel that are dark, and many unsavory creatures are lurking about. There is fog everywhere and the inexperienced traveler can become quickly lost and confused. But if you journey to the land of the Ancestors, you will see a quiet place of light and happiness. The dead are kept in a place of beauty and peace. I am not sure if Hela created this wonderful place or the Ancestors did. However it happened, contrary to some of the poems written about this place, in my experience it is a place where the Ancestors are happy.

Traveling down to Helheim is one of my favorite places in the Underworld. Like the myths and legends say, things are not what they seem. I first find myself at the great golden bridge that crosses a river to the great hall of Hela. The hall, to me, looks more like a fortress than a Nordic hall, but this could just be my perception. Once I cross the bridge, the gate opens to a dark a gloomy castle. But because I have had many conversations with Hel, I know the secret of getting into the realm of the Ancestors. There is a veil that the traveler must open. Much like opening the veil in a pagan ritual. Once the veil is open a castle of light, music, and merriment is revealed. I often see men and women feasting at a great table. Why should those in Valhalla have all the fun? The great castle glows with such a wonderful shimmering light that I am often struck with the beauty of it all. Deep in the center of the great castle, there is a great cavern that goes to the depths below. If you look down, you will see that the great castle spirals down deep to the vastness of the Underworld. At the bottom is a great well used for magick, healing, and scrying. When I am wandering through the land of the ancestors here, I often enjoy the beautiful countryside and see many houses and cottages that the ancestors have. I can feel the presence of Hela in the land, trees, and mountains here. Her grace is everywhere. I recall one time when I found some of the villagers doing a ritual in Hela's name. "Was there a special occasion?" I asked. One of the ladies chuckled and replied, "In this place we honor the power and protection of Hela always. She is our mother, and we love her."

The Celtic Otherworld/Underworld

One of the most mysterious and strange aspects of the Underworld appears in the myths and legends of the Celts. The Celts did not necessarily see the Underworld in the way modern Neo-Shamans do. How they see the Underworld more closely relates to how indigenous people see it. The Underworld is on, in, and around the physical world. They call it The Otherworld. The Celtic Otherworld is not as neatly organized, or rather, separated, like the Three Shamanic Worlds we are used to hearing about. The Celtic Otherworld contains the lands of the dead, nature spirits and the gods. It is more complicated, and at the same time, easier to understand than it sounds. This is the beauty and the Mystery of the Celtic Otherworld. At times, the realms of the Celtic nature spirits, gods, and the dead bleed into one another and you can see how all three interact. In Celtic myth and story, we often see that the hero or heroine frequently stumbles across the Otherworld by accident. Usually, they are not looking for anything in particular. The myths are filled with castles that appear and disappear, faery hills that lead into the land of the fey, and places of the dead that lead straight to their realm. We will focus primarily on the journeys of the dead and the powers of the Otherworld in how it relates to our topic of the Underworld.

Anwyyn

This is the Celtic Underworld according to the Welsh people. It is similar to the idea of the Celtic Otherworld; however, the primary difference is that it is "underground" or in a place called The Hollow Hill. The Hollow Hill is a grave mound or burial mound that houses the bodies of people of importance. It is called "Hollow" because it is a sacred place of burial. In myth, it is also the "hollow" because there is another world inside, or rather, an entrance to another world. The grave mound is a portal or gateway to the Land of the Dead. It is also thought to be a gateway to the Welsh land of faery. It must be clear that the Ancestors and the Faery Folk are not the same entities as some authors suggest. They are two completely different families of beings. The grave mound is a portal to the Otherworld and not the Otherworld itself. Think of it like a "spiritual train station" that can take you to other destinations. Although, in Celtic belief, if one dies than they may live in the world of faery if they wish, and of course, if they faery folk allow it. There are indeed magical people who have Faery Blood or who have developed a deep kinship with the Faeries. When this happens, they may be invited to dwell among the Faeries after death. One such story relates to the author and folklorist, Rev. Robert Kirk. Kirk was a minister and folklorist in the 17th century in England. He wrote many stories and tales of the Fey folk and nature spirits. He would often visit the Faery mounds at night. One night, his body was found dead on such a hill. It was believed that the Faeries rewarded Kirk by taking him to live in the Faery mounds forever.

Anwyyn is a place of magick, renewal, and mystery. It is a place where the dead can rest and find peace. It does have a mystery of its own and there are many tales of people crossing a Hollow Hill and "accidentally" finding themselves in the Welsh Underworld. Once there, they find many strange things such as magical creatures and vast amounts of treasure. When they return to the world of the living, their lives are changed forever. Like most descriptions of the Underworld from around the world, Anwyyn is a place that tests the character and Will of each individual so that they may pass further into the depths of mystery and spiritual evolution . This is done because if you do not find your Divine Will and face your fears, you cannot tread deeper into the mysteries of death and the dark gods and spirits. Once you pass the tests, you are granted a greater understanding of the Universe and are able to take these invaluable teachings back to the Midworld to heal yourself and others; and perhaps to bring a greater understanding of the difficult (but inevitable) phenomenon of death to people.

Anwyyn is ruled by the Lord of the Dead, Gwyn ap Nudd. He has been described sometimes as a horned or a cloaked man who comes up through the Hollow Hill during the Wild Hunt to hunt down the souls of the dead that will forever dwell deep within his realm. Those who have "the sight" have told tales of seeing the Hill open up to release the terrifying figure of a cloaked man and his ghostly train looking for souls. This does sound scary indeed! In reality, it is more like a Father gathering his children to take them home in order for them to become happy in the Otherworld. The living often find the dead and the Underworld frightening because we fear death and its mysteries. We will not understand these dreadful things fully until it is our time to be gathered up by the Cloaked One, to be taken down into the Hallow Hill Forever, but we might gain a glimpse of these mysteries by exploring the Underworld.

Traveling into the Hollow Hill, for me, is quite different than traveling to Hades or Hel. By my home in Chicago, there is a manmade large hill (I suppose all Hollow Hills are manmade) named Cricket Hill.

I use the hill to connect astrally to all hallowed hills. Once connected to all hills, I use the hill as a gateway into the Underworld realm of Gwyn Up Nudd. When I arrive in the Underworld I am surrounded by a large forest. The forest is thick, and I know there are small family villages of ancestors deep within. Once I journey through the terrain, I am in a beautiful countryside which is in the middle ages. I see castles and fortresses all through the land. I journey further to the castle of Gwyn Up Nudd. His castle is also an entrance to star gates. The Ancestors who live in this land are happy and enjoy the comings and goings of the faery folk that sometime come to this part of the Underworld. I do not have a formal relationship with Gwyn Up Nudd like other Underworld Deities, but I am still invited to see parts of his Underworld that many do not get to see. I believe this is because he recognizes me to be a seasoned Underworld traveler. Or perhaps I humor him in some way. Either way, he shows me the enchanting land where he keeps the dead safe and happy.

The Celtic Islands of the Otherworld

The Irish Celts looked to the west at the setting sun and saw that the sun sank under the sea and brought about the night. Sea travel had many dangers such as storms, starvation, and getting lost out on the great ocean. The sea, to the Irish Celts was the Under/Otherworld itself, the Great Mystery. The sea seemed to be the edge of the world; a place the dead would go for their final journey into the arms of the Otherworld. To journey into the realm of the sea was to journey far into the mysteries of death.

The Irish Celts viewed the Otherworld as having many islands in the west. The further one traveled into the Islands of the Otherworld, the deeper into the mysteries one would go. There are many tales of heroes traveling to the islands of the Otherworld in search of knowledge, power, and adventure. There are also tales of heroes finding themselves off-course from their destination to be led into the depth of the Otherworld islands. These tales told of strange places, creatures, and people who taught the hero many valuable lessons about life, death, and spirituality.

When working with the Otherworld Islands, you may explore these wonderful places to find powerful and magical things such as the secrets of magical abilities, the powers of the ancestors, and the forces of the Otherworld just as the ancient Celtic heroes did. You may also use the islands to practice your own personal transition to the afterlife if you follow a Celtic cosmology. I find that the Celtic Islands of the Otherworld can seem familiar to the Underworld realms of the Egyptians, Maya, and Tibetans. The islands can be linked to the subconscious mind and we may "practice" the art of dying or simply learn about ourselves in this fantastic journey.

One popular Celtic myth is the "The Voyage of Bran Son of Febal." In this Irish saga, Bran meets a woman who is from the Otherworld. She tells him tales of the wonders of the islands there, of the joys and beauties, and the beautiful women that await him and his traveling companions if they will but journey there. Bran takes the journey by sea but is met by a man who calls himself Manannan, Son of Lir. The reader knows this man to be the Irish God of the Under/Otherworld and the Lord of the Dead. He tells Bran and his crew about the journey ahead. Most of the tale was written in the 1100s so it has a very Christian slant, referring to Christ, Adam, and Eve. Manannan tells Bran of the mysteries of the island Otherworld and the prophecy of he and his men. Bran sails further and finds the island of women where his men stay for a time. But as we have discussed before, time in the Under/

Otherworld is not like time in the physical plane. It has its own rules if it has any rules at all. Bran eventually convinces his men to sail back to the land they came from. One of his crewmen, excited about returning home, leapt from the ship onto the land where he immediately turned into ash. Bran and his men had not known how long they were in the Otherworld. Once returning home, time caught up with them. Bran turned his ship around and sailed back into the Otherworld islands to forever become part of the mysteries.

There is another tale called "The Voyage of Maelduinn." This tale is similar to "The Voyage of Bran," however, this story goes deeper into the mysteries of the Island Otherworld. The poem offers more details about each of the islands and the experiences of Maelduinn and his crew. The crew discovers islands with strange and wondrous creatures. They find giant ants, birds, cannibal horses, the Ancestors, mists, and the island of women. Each of these islands takes Maelduinn and his crew deeper and deeper into the Otherworld. Some of the islands and creatures they encounter are life threatening. Other islands are there to challenge their will. Once they overcome an island, their spirits are better prepared to face the next challenge of the Otherworld.

As you can see, the islands may be linked to the deeper realms of the Underworld and the subconscious. An interesting thought may be that the Underworld is the subconscious of the Source of all things, or the Creator. If we look back to the analogy that God/dess created the Universe in Their image, then perhaps our subconscious is linked to the subconscious of the Universe. I personally believe that when we journey into the Underworld, we are doing so astrally and spiritually as well as traveling into the depths of our own minds. I like to think of this as a mirror of the Universe. In Buddhist belief, all aspects of the world and the Universe are simply reflections of our own minds and emotions. I believe this to be also true with the three worlds. With this theory, it is safe to say that by journeying through the islands of the Celtic Otherworld we are also discovering the deeper mysteries of ourselves and aspects of our deeper psyche. The entities we discover in the Underworld appear however we hope or fear them to be. Remember, energy is energy. It is through our personal mental lenses that these entities appear the way that they do. However, many people who have never spoken to each other will return from an Underworld journey with a similar description of the same entity, god, or spirit. One reason is that our culture has many of the same myths, beliefs, and experiences. For example, when we think of a beautiful woman, many American men may conjure up the image of a slender blond with large breasts. Thus, in the Underworld, when a spirit wants to portray themselves as a beautiful woman, the spirit may appear as a slender blond with large breasts. When other people from around the world think of someone beautiful, the image will be different than what is considered standard American beauty. The important thing here is not to dwell on what spirits should look like, but what they look like to you and what teachings and lessons are you learning from it.

I will say that not all lessons that present themselves need to be learned right away. There are times when the lessons in the Underworld come about it is because the energies want you to begin the process of learning and growing as a spiritual being. Some lessons take a lifetime to learn. Go at the pace you feel is right for you. If you are working with a teacher or a group, discuss what is happening with the other people you are working with and come up with a plan of action.

Exercise: Exploring the Underworld

1. Lie comfortably and take a deep breath. Begin to relax your body, emotions, mind with each passing breath.
2. State your intention to explore the realms of the dead. You can pick anyone from any culture you like. I would advise reading some of the myths and stories before you take on your journey.
3. Visualize a bright light beginning at your feet and spiraling clockwise, spiral up the entirety of your body.
4. Energetically feel your astral body being transported to your destination.
5. Once you feel you have arrived at your destination, see the spiraling light unravel itself going from your head down to your feet, revealing your destination.
6. Enjoy your Underworld journey. Remember to be polite and gracious to anyone or anything you meet. If you come up to an impasse, try to go around or try again another day. If any offerings are required ask yourself if you are willing to give the expected offering. If so, give it astrally in the Underworld. Once you return home remember to give the offerings in the physical plane. You can leave it on your altar, on the land, or in a lake, river, or ocean.
7. To return home, simply visualize the spiraling light again (steps 3-5).

Place of Rejuvenation

The Underworld is not only a place of the dead and great, powerful beings. It is also a place of healing, rejuvenation, and renewal. There are many myths of the Underworld containing places that heal the sick and purify the body of disease. It is a place of transformation. The most common theme throughout many cultures is the ability of the Underworld to take a person, spirit, or god and help them evolve into something better and greater than they were when they first started their Underworld journey. In almost all cultures, the soul of a person enters the Underworld and is sent on a series of quests. Each quest is literally a test of the person's integrity, honor, love, and valor. As one goes through the Underworld, each quest is more challenging than the next. This is especially true for the Egyptian and Mayan cosmologies. But it is also interesting to note that the Egyptian and Mayan cultures that were among the world's first to create large-scale buildings for the dead to be placed in. The purpose of these quests is to see what the person's spirit is made of. These journeys that the hero must make are designed in such a way to mold the soul. In almost all the stories concerning Underworld tests, the hero does not even know how strong he or she really is until they have defeated the challenges they most feared.

There are many places in the Underworld where the hero is able to eat and drink magical food and water to restore themselves back into health. In the myth of King Arthur, he is taken to the Otherworldly Isle of Avalon so that he may be restored back to health. However, in the story, he must remain in Avalon as a magical hero until Britain needs him the most. It is often interesting to note that when the Underworld grants you favors or magical power there is almost always a certain amount of energy exchange expected in return. In some myths, the spirits or gods ask the hero to go on a journey to retrieve some magical item. Other myths tell of how the spirits of the Underworld ask the hero to use their new powers in the name of the Underworld or certain gods.

The Underworld is a powerful place for healing and transformation. It is important to realize that the more you travel through the Underworld, the more interested and invested in you that the gods and spirits become, and the more they will want to help you with your spiritual development. As a rule, I never accept a gift from a god or entity I am not familiar with. Myths are full of tales of heroes who blindly accept gifts and powers without understanding what was going to happen to them. The hero would later find out that the gift was either too powerful for them to manage properly, or it was a curse in disguise. J.R.R. Tolkien's *Lord of the Rings* is a great example of this. In the story, nine great kings were given magick rings that promised power but would later only serve the purpose of evil by enslaving them to the Dark Lord who assisted in the making of the rings.

The best way to approach this situation is to ask the spirit or god exactly what is going to happen when the gift is accepted. They will not take offense to questions such as these as long as you are polite! If you do not understand or are unwilling to perform the expectation, then it is wise to decline the gift. However, if the powers of the gift are something you are able and willing to do, I see no harm in accepting the gift. When in doubt, ask the advice of your personal Ancestors, spirit animal, and spirits.

Exercise:
Finding Your Underworld Place of Healing

1. Use the previous exercises on astral projection and journeying to enter the Underworld.
2. Find your Midworld Center.
3. Call upon your Spirit animal guide
4. Visualize or find an Underworld entrance and ask your spirit animal to lead you down into the Underworld to find a place of healing and rejuvenation.
5. Follow your spirit animal down into the Underworld. Again, it can appear as if you are going through the vast roots of the World

Tree, tunnels deep into the Earth, staircases down, or even a giant slide. You may use any means that works for you.

6. Once in the Underworld, again ask your spirit animal to lead you to a place of healing and rejuvenation. You may also call upon your Underworld teacher to show you the way.

7. At this point, you may see great oceans, rivers, wells, forests, fires, or caverns. You may even be led to a castle, cottage, or some other dwelling—perhaps even one that has been described or which you have read about from the mythologies above. Usually, places of healing have a guardian or guide of some sort. Explain your intentions to heal and learn about healing to the guardian. There may be times when the guardian asks for payment or a favor. This is not always the case. If the payment is coins, leave some coins for the spirit in the physical world. If it is a favor, make sure you are able and willing to perform the favor in the time requested. If you are not able to make the payment or favor, kindly say so and ask your spirit animal and teacher to find you another place of healing.

8. The best places of healing are ones that you are led to that are "just for you." No payment or favor necessary. Remember this place. Perhaps give it a name. You can come back to this place whenever you choose for healing.

9. There are times when the totem and teacher cannot or will not take you to a place of healing. This is not a punishment or a "failure" in your journeying. It may simply mean that you must learn and experience more before you are given this wonderful gift.

10. Once you have found your healing place, thank your totem and teacher and give offerings.

11. Journal about your experience.

The Six Bardos

In Tibetan Buddhism, the cosmology is broken up into Bardos. Bardo means "in-between" or can mean a duration of time in the universe. There are six Bardos.

1. The Natural Bardo of This Life
2. The Bardo of Dream
3. The Bardo of Meditation
4. The Painful Bardo of Dying
5. The Luminous Bardo of Dharmata
6. The Karmic Bardo of Becoming

Each Bardo is intended for spiritual and Karmic teachings and lessons. In Buddhist philosophy, the goal of each individual is "liberation." Liberation in the Buddhist sense is to liberate one's self from the Karmic wheel of life, death, and rebirth. Many of those liberated, having attained Buddha consciousness, join with the supreme deity. Some of those liberated reincarnate to enjoy a life free of hardships, while others return to become gurus, teachers, and healers.

I believe that it would only benefit the student of magick, death, and healing to learn about the Bardos and learn each karmic lesson that each one has to offer. It is interesting to me that Buddhists believe that the Otherworld is pure energy and the experiences that we have in each of the Bardos is a creation of our own minds, spirits, and emotions. We may dwell in a place of bliss and love or a place of hell and torment, depending on how well we are able to control our thoughts and emotions, especially our fears. This is not to say that the spirits of the Universe do not press us to learn and grow even more. But how we do so, is up to us. This resonates with me in the sense that there is no punishment in the Otherworlds, only opportunities for growth and evolution. Our soul, or spirit, is designed to evolve and grow; to find "enlightenment". Our soul is programmed to seek out opportunities for spiritual growth. It may be through suffering or through life experience. How we see these experiences is completely up to us.

The Natural Bardo of This Life

This is the Earth plane. It is the life that we are living now. This Bardo creates many opportunities to learn, evolve, and grow from daily living. If one has Karma to work off from a previous life, then this is a wonderful time to do so. Buddhist scripture teaches of a life lived of virtue, meditation, devotion to deity, and good deeds create good energy and Karma so that at the time of death it will be easy to recognize the energies of wisdom and deity so that they may become liberated.

The Bardo of Dream

This Bardo is our dream state during sleep. This can be a gateway into the Bardo of Dharmata (the Otherworld) but is not the Otherworld itself. It is here that the dedicated student of Buddhism may learn how to become lucid in their dreams and learn to control the energy (astral) body. When this is perfected, it is easy to navigate through the Otherworld after death and discover the energies of wisdom and deity so that they may become liberated. This is a discipline usually passed from teacher to student, however, some people who have had several lives may remember the skill of the dream Bardo.

The Bardo of Meditation

This Bardo is the state of mind and consciousness during meditation. Through discipline and self-mastery, we can learn how to free ourselves from attachment, move beyond false ego, and learn to become virtuous and have an open heart. When this is perfected, fear and delusion of the subconscious are conquered. When we die, fear and delusions of the Earth Bardo are manifested in the Bardo of Dharmata. When we conquer fears, it is easy to navigate through the spirit world and recognize wisdom and deity.

The Painful Bardo of Dying

This Bardo is the process of dying itself. It is said that dying begins when we become aware that time is short, and preparations must be made. It is here that attachments to material things are released. It is also a time to practice forgiveness for those people who have hurt you and to ask forgiveness from those you have hurt. It is the time to clear out negative energies and prepare your mind for the journey ahead. One also practices for the final thought at the point of death. If a person's feelings at death are negative, then they will find themselves in a negative place; if positive, then a positive place. At the point of death, the physical and energetic properties of the body dissipate, and the consciousness (mind) goes on to the next Bardo.

The Luminous Bardo of Dharmata

This is the Otherworld itself. In this Bardo the spirit is faced with his or her own mind and subconscious. The spirits, or Buddhas, appear in many forms and it is up to each individual to recognize the deities and join with them. If one has much fear, delusion, and bad karma, they will misunderstand the fierceness of the gods as evil and they will stay away from them. It is only through recognizing the Buddhas for what they are that someone finds liberation. This Bardo gives several opportunities for the dead to find liberation. As the days progress, the spirits become more and more fierce so that they are perceived as monsters and demons.

For the Buddhist, they literally create their own hell. This is done because the energies of this Bardo are trying to get the dead to give in to fear and find liberation. After many days, if the dead person has not found liberation, then they will journey to the next Bardo.

The Karmic Bardo of Becoming

This Bardo is also in the spirit world, but its purpose has changed. Instead of being liberated, the focus turns to reincarnation. The idea is that because there was so much negativity, fear, and lack of virtue, it will take the spirit another life to learn to be virtuous and not fearful. There are several ways this can happen. Different colored lights will appear. The white lights are the top heavens where the deities live, the red lights are the lower heavens where the jealous gods live, the blue lights are where the humans live, the green lights are where the animals live, the yellow lights are where the hungry ghosts live, and the pale grey lights are the hell worlds where the demons live. According to your thoughts, actions, and deeds, you will be attracted to the appropriate lights. It is said that the blue lights of the world of humans are best to work off negative karma and learn virtue, but there are lessons in each world that will teach liberation.

When you begin your Underworld journeys you will see many strange yet wonderful things. Myths from different cultures will give different examples of how to enter the world below. There may be differences, but they are all equally as valid. There is the traditional view of Neo-shamanism that the Underworld is entered through the roots of the great world tree that take you into a spiritual Universe below. That is certainly a good way to begin, but there are many other ways to enter the Underworld. Once there, the journey may seem odd and disorienting; but by practicing, your journey you will become an one as an accomplished spirit worker indeed. As we are learning, the Underworld has terrain that is much like ours here in the Midworld. But do not be fooled. This is a place where what you thought was up is really down and vice versa. The dead are here, and many cultures tell their stories. Some of these places are beautiful and some may never want to leave, but then again, perhaps they may not be able to. The realms of the dead are rarely ventured to for a reason. However, these places also have treasures of wisdom, power, and our loved ones long gone. As we go forward in this book, we will see all the wonder and adventure these places have waiting for us.

3
The Hell Worlds

The Hells

Most of the Western world is used to hearing the word "Hell." We know from Christian literature that Hell is a place of torment and burning for all eternity. We know that Hell is the dwelling place of evil beings. We know that Hell is a place we want to avoid at all costs. From what we learn from Christian mythology, it is a place that has no purpose except to punish. Upon reading myths from other cultures, we can see that the authors who have translated the myths into English borrowed our English word "Hell" to describe the places in their cosmology that are places of purification and testing grounds for future existence on the material plane. Clearly, there is a vast difference in meaning here.

Some cultures believe that for each person, life is meant to be an evolution of the spirit/soul and a time to learn lessons. These philosophies are well aware that our human minds and bodies must go through life on their own paths with both triumphs and failures. Most cultures do not believe in the concept of sin, but do believe that self-doubt, sadness, anger, and jealousy leave negative energy on the soul/spirit. This energy must be purified before the person can join the

Ancestors and gods in the Realm of the Dead. This purification is done through traveling in spirit to the hells and going through trials and tests. This is part of the "Hero's Journey" that we talked about in the previous chapters. The hero journeys through the Hells as part of his adventure to bring himself empowerment and spiritual evolution.

Some people who go through these trials have been studying spirituality for years. They have read the myths and learned from books and teachers. These people easily go through the trials and quickly move on to be with their Ancestors. Other people who have quite a bit of negativity imprinted on their spirit/souls have a harder time with the trials. Sometimes they must spend a great deal of time with the trials trying to make their way through their specific "hell." Sometimes, they do not make it through the first time, and have to try many times before they are successful in their quest.

It is important to realize that it does not matter how much life experience someone has had at this point. Nor does it matter how many "bad" things the person has done. Good and bad are concepts made up by a human earthly society and have little to do with the afterlife and the Underworld. The gods, spirits, and energies are more concerned with how much you are able to let go and move on. They want to know how well you are able to accept responsibility for (and learn from) your mistakes! This is the true meaning of going through the tests and trials with a pure heart. After the tests are complete, the spirit/soul sometimes re-incarnates if more lessons on Earth are to be learned. If they have reached a certain point in their spiritual development they may be able to pass on to the place of the Ancestors and perhaps become a spirit guide for people living on Earth. At this point, it is not for me to tell you what to believe, but rather to clarify the beliefs of other spiritual philosophies. Later in your Underworld journeys, I encourage you to travel to these places and test out how much negative energy you are retaining in your soul.

Each culture tests the spirit in a different way. The trials and tests in the Underworld have cultural meaning to each society. They are also based on your subconscious and the negative energy that you retain. You may not even be aware of the negativity onto which you are holding. But, once you are in the Underworld, your subconscious becomes like a film projector that projects your deepest hopes, fears, and desires into the powerful energies available. The pain and suffering that you refuse to let go of, or perhaps do not know how to let go of, will manifest. In some cultures, this energy manifests as sinister lords of chaos chasing you through darkness. In other cultures, the energy manifests as wild animals and beasts that wish to eat you. These scenarios provide the spirits with the opportunity to face their darkest parts in order to move on and purify themselves of the negativity. In Buddhism, there are many meditation techniques that will help you understand these energies. Buddhism teaches us that we may learn to deal with them in life so once we pass beyond the veil of life and death the monsters that chase us are easier to handle.

The Maya

They ancient Maya were a Native South American culture that lived on the Yucatan peninsula. Very early on, they learned the magick of agriculture. The most important food to them was maize, or corn. Their cosmology was similar to other pagan and native tribes in some ways, but very different in others. They built temples, had a system of government, and had priests that maintained the sacred rites and sought out spirits to aid the tribe. They waged wars with enemies and used the captives as sacrifices to their gods in order to preserve their people. The

Maya flourished for hundreds of years. In the 8th Century the power of the Maya began to wane and in the 9th Century the great powerful empire was but an ember of the once mighty people of the Yucatan.

Beliefs

The Maya believed that the Universe has three worlds. The physical world or Midworld, an Upperworld, and an Underworld. There was an energy force that made up the entire Mayan Universe that is called *ch'ulel*. This "life" energy was much like the Chinese concept of Chi or the Indian idea of *prana*. *Ch'ulel* was the life force that gave life-energy to all of creation. Without it, the Universe could not exist; nothing would be. *Ch'ulel* came from the three Mayan worlds and at the same time it kept everything in motion. For the Maya, the Universe, including those parts of it that were not physical, was ever changing and evolving. *Ch'ulel* gave life to the crops and helped them grow. It also gave the Maya "good energy" for everyday life, government, and war. If the *Ch'ulel* were to run out in the physical world, then the Mayan world would no longer exist. *Ch'ulel* also gave energy to the Ancestors to help them have influence in the physical world and it gave energy to the gods to assist them with helping humans to manifest a healthy and vital existence. From time to time *Ch'ulel* would become depleted. The largest known source of *Ch'ulel* in the physical world was blood.

It was thought to be a divine act to sacrifice a human being in the name of the gods and the Mayan civilization. They believed that the gods themselves created the Universe through blood sacrifice. It is said in the *Popul Vu* that the Universe was created when the gods stuck large needles through their penises and the blood spilling helped to create the cosmos. The sacrifice was chosen from a sort of "divine" game that was held in the sacred ball courts of the Mayan temples. It was similar to our racket ball. On one side were the gods of life and on the other side were the gods of death and disease. The gods of life always won, so by default the losing team was dubbed the "gods of death and disease". These men were then usually decapitated in the temple and their blood, which contained much *Ch'ulel*, would spill into a hole in the temple floor down onto the Earth below (the Underworld). The *Ch'ulel* would then be given to the Underworld gods to use for the benefit of the people and the Earth around them.

In his book, *The Shaman's Secret,* Douglas Gillette states, "The Maya shamans believed that all deaths, but especially those of the authentic human beings, are, in their essence, "sacrificial" deaths. In these sacrificial deaths human beings give back to the gods what the gods, through their own sacrifices, have given them - blood for blood, tears for rain, flesh for corn, life for life, being for being."

He goes on to say that the Maya beliefs surrounding these customs were shared by not only those who carried out the sacrifices, but by the people who were sacrificed as well. Pain and suffering were a natural way of life, and while the victims did not want to die, most of them tried to do so with honor and dignity knowing that they were helping restore the life force of their people. The victim's names were recorded and held in great honor.

The Mayan Underworld was called Xibalba. It was the realm of the god of death who was called One and Seven Death. Sometimes this deity was perceived as one god and other times as two separate gods. They were the leaders of the Underworld. Xibalba had many spirits and "hells" for the soul to travel through.

Road to Xibalba

When the Maya died, it was thought that their spirits or souls would become a traveler in the Underworld. Throughout their lives, they were taught about the mysteries of the Underworld. They were taught about all the dangerous trials that awaited them. In essence, they prepared for death their entire lives. They were also taught to live a spiritual life as best they could, because doing so would better prepare them for the trials in Xibalba. Death was a sacred and necessary act for the balance of creation. But for the Maya, it was not about being "good" in life, it was about preparing the soul for the onslaught of "hells" that were meant to purify and test the soul.

Once they died, their journey would begin. They would start by going down over the edge of a steep slope, then they would descend until they reached the mouth where the canyons changed. The canyons were named Rustling Canyon and Gurgling Canyon. After traveling through the vastness of the canyons they would pass through Scorpion Rapids and then on to a river of blood, called Blood River. Then they journeyed on to a river of Pus after which they encountered a crossroads. The crossroads were named after the sacred colors of the Maya: the Red Road and the Black Road. Then there were the White Road and the Yellow Road. We must remember that the Maya were not trying to repulse the spirit traveler but to explain that in the world of death, there existed the things that brought death or the symptoms of illness that led to death in the Underworld. These things were also part of the trials that lay ahead. The spirit traveler had to be brave and put his or her fears aside and continue across the terrain.

Once you came to the crossroads, the Black Road would speak, "I am the road to Xibalba". The spirit traveler was taught in life which way to go. They knew to go down the Black road to reach the Mayan

Underworld. It is helpful to know that the soul traveler was not completely alone on the journey. There were allies that accompanied them upon their quest. One of the allies was the mosquito. This creature could be used as a spy in the Underworld. It could be sent ahead to find out what dangers awaited. This was helpful because the gods and spirits of Xibalba, also known as the Lords of Xibalba, wanted to very much confuse and frighten the traveler. The Lords of Xibalba would use manikins to fool travelers to confuse them along the way. The manikins looked just like the Maya people and the traveler would think that they had found someone to help them along their path. When the traveler found out that they were tricked, it would further the sense of isolation and the realization that they had to travel the dark paths alone. They were also pranksters and loved to play mean tricks on travelers, such as giving them a hot seat. When the traveler grew tired and tried to sit down, the seats were scalding hot! The Lords of Xibalba took great delight in doing this. To the reader, these pranks may seem childish, but we should remember that the journey was frightening to the newly dead and everything could be perceived as a danger. These little tricks were nothing compared to the trials that were soon to come. To turn back with fear was to show the Underworld gods that one was not ready for re-incarnation or spiritual evolution.

Houses of Xibalba

The goal for the spirit traveler was reincarnation, or evolution of the spirit, into the spirit worlds and the realm of the Ancestors. The soul had to be tested and purified. To do this, there were "hells" or "houses." These realms taught the soul what it needed to move forward. It was hoped that every soul, because of its proper training in life, would gracefully pass through the houses. If a soul failed its trials, then a state of limbo or a netherworld was its destination. The houses themselves were conditions of human suffering that the soul traveler had to confront and deal with, so that they would understand the purpose of life, suffering, sacrifice, death, and their own spiritual resurrection.

The first house that was encountered was Dark House. This was a house with only darkness in it. Here, travelers were given a torch. The torch represented spiritual illumination. Travelers were also given a cigar. The traveler was told that the torch and cigar must not go out! This was the trial that tested spiritual development and the trueness of the soul. The torch was a direct link to the "light" of the Maya spirit. If it went out, then the traveler was not ready to move forward.

The second house encountered was the Razor (Blade) House. This house was filled with razor blades swinging back and forth. Being that this was the last house before the continuation of the soul to reincarnation or evolution of spirit, this was the place where the last of the unwanted aspects of the soul were cut away. This may have been a violent cutting, but it was necessary. To move beyond into the realm of spirit, all fear, pain, and suffering had be irrevocably purged and the lessons fully learned. This was the trial that cut away negative aspects of the soul and taught the understanding that violence must have an outlet lest it find unhealthy means of expressing itself.

From the Razor House, travelers move to the Cold (Rattling) House. As the name implies, the house was very cold inside with heavy drafts that made whistling sounds. There were also the chattering sounds of hail falling upon the roof of the house. The soul traveler had to keep warm with its own internal fire. This was the trial that tested the ability to keep the inner flame kindled. The inner fire may have been the passion for living, in right relation with one's community.

The next house was Jaguar House. The jaguars jostled one another around and were crowded together. These mighty beasts were violent and hungry and had the potential to devour the sojourner's soul. This was the trial that tested the ability to not fight death, but to let the forces of death feed on the spirit.

Then there was the Fire House. The fires were those of purification which burned away the old self, especially those parts of the ego that did not propel the soul forward. This was the house that was similar to the Christian concept of a fiery hell. In Christian hell too, if you look deep enough into the symbolism, you find the "destruction" of a sinful or false ego. It is the purification of hell that allows the soul to purge itself of impurity so that it might go forth on an evolutionary road. The Fire House also tested the ability of one to keep the mind "cool" so that it did not give into the fires of anger and rage.

Last was house is the Bat House which was filled only with bats. They represented the terrible aspect of death that mortals had no power over. To fight this house was futile. In fact, to fight any of the houses went against the very nature of the aspect of the Universe that they represented. The bats gave a sense of dread and fear. Their shrieks were deafening. This house represented the essence of fear in the journey of death. It was terrible, but inevitable. This was the trial that tested the ability to give in to the cosmic flow of death and transformation and give it what it wanted.

One and Seven Hanahpu

There were two gods of the Maya named One and Seven Hanahpu. One Hanahpu had a wife and fathered children, but Seven Hanahpu was to forever remain a boy. These two gods were very good and were great seers. One and Seven Hanahpu taught the sons of One Hanahpu many arts and crafts. The sons, in turn, taught these gifts to humanity.

One and Seven Hanahpu spent their days throwing dice and playing ball. However, they chose to play their games over the road to Xibalba, the Mayan Underworld. One and Seven Death heard these games and were angry at the disrespect that One and Seven Hanahpu were showing them. One and Seven Death decided to destroy them by inviting them down into the Underworld and playing a ball game.

As One and Seven Hanahpu traveled down to Xibalba they passed over great Canyons and mighty rapids. They were able to pass through a River of Blood and a River of Pus. They passed unharmed! They then came to a crossroads. A red road, a black road, a yellow road, and a white road. The black road spoke and told them to take the black road to Xibalba. They then came to the Lords of Xibalba. This meant their defeat, because as they went to greet the lords, they did not know that this was a trick. These were not the lords of the Underworld—they were manikins. When they finally did meet the Lords of Xibalba, instead of granting them a seat, they were tricked again and given hot rocks to sit on.

One and Seven Hanahpu were unaware that the Underworld was filled with tests of torment. They were sent to Dark House and given one cigar each with a torch to light them. They were told to keep the cigars intact, but in the morning when One and Seven Death came to retrieve them One and Seven Hanahpu explained that the cigars had been smoked up. They had failed the test. One and Seven Death killed One and Seven Hanahpu because they had failed the tests of Xibalba. The bodies were buried over the ball court and the head of One Hanahpu was placed in the fork of a cabash tree. This tree became a magical tree of the Underworld.

Hanahpu and Xblanque in the Underworld

After some time, in the Underworld, A maiden named Blood Moon, came up to the magical tree where One Hanahpu's head was placed. She had heard that the fruit of the tree was sweet and wanted it. She asked the head of One Hanahpu for the fruit, but instead of giving her the fruit, he spat in her hand. The spittle disappeared at once and Blood Moon became pregnant with the essence of One Hanahpu. The Lords of the Underworld wanted to kill Blood Moon, so she fled to the world above and lived with the Mother of One Hanahpu. She later gave birth to Hanahpu and Xblanque.

Hanahpu and Xblanque grew up to be immensely powerful and crafty. They loved to play ball on the road to Xibalba just as their father did before, and, just as before, the Lords of Xibalba did not like all the noise from above and invited the boys to come down to the Underworld to play a ball game with the intention of inevitably sacrificing them!

So down went Hanahpu and Xblanque to Xibalba. They passed through the dark canyons and passed over the River of Blood and the River of Pus. The found themselves at the crossroads again. They already knew to go down the Black Road. They also knew about the tricks that the Lords of Xibalba liked to play. They summoned Mosquito and had him bite the lords so that they would know their names. The Mosquito bit the Lords, and they all said their names in turn which were One Death, Seven Death, Scab Stripper, Blood Gatherer, Demon of Pus, Demon of Justice, Bone Scepter, Skull Scepter, Packstrap, Bloody Teeth, Bloody Claws, and Wing. Hanahpu and Xblanque walked by the first Lords of the Underworld they encountered; they were not fooled by the manikins. They named each of the actual lords when they met them and, in this way, had power over them. They did not fall for any of the tricks. They did not even sit on the hot rocks.

They were then taken to Dark House. Hanahpu and Xblanque were given cigars and a torch and were told not to let them burn up. Instead of lighting the cigars, they stuffed fireflies in the cigars to give the lords the illusion that they were smoking them. In the morning, The lords realized what had happened and knew that they had been defeated. That day, they played ball and the lords tried to kill them with a knife, but the boys saw the knife and knew they were being tricked. Despite this attempt on their lives, the boys agreed to stay another night. On the second night, they were taken to Razor House. The house was filled with knives and was supposed to slice them up, but the boys spoke to the knives and convinced them that they would rather have animal flesh. The knives stopped their attack, and the boys spent the night in Razor House unharmed. The next day, they played ball again and had a tie. The lords asked them to stay another night. This time, Hanahpu and Xblanque were taken to Cold House. Cold House was full of cold winds and hail. The boys defeated the house by shutting the cold out. They closed the windows and doors and would not let in the cold spirits. The Lords of Xibalba were very angry. Next, they were taken to Jaguar House. The boys said to the jaguars that they should not eat them, but rather gnaw on bones. The boys then transformed themselves into bones and the jaguars gnawed on them but did not devour them. The next day, they transformed back into boys and the Lords of the Underworld were defeated again. Next, they were taken to Fire House. The fires were supposed to burn them up, but they left the house once again unharmed! Last, they were taken to Bat House where bats great and small shrieked and swooped down on them all night long. Xblanque asked Hanahpu to check outside the window to see if it was dawn yet. When Hanahpu peeked out of the window a bat flew down and bit off his head and the head of Hanahpu rolled outside on the ground. In despair, Xblanque summoned forth all the animals and asked them to run and get the food they ate. After inspecting all the food, he found a squash. He transformed the squash into a temporary head for Hanahpu and brought him back to life! That morning, the boys and the Lords of Death played ball, using the head of Hanahpu as a ball! Finally, Hanahpu and Xblanque won the ball game and the head of Hanahpu was restored to his body. This was how the Lords of Xibalba were defeated.

Egyptian Underworld
Osiris and Isis (Egyptian)

Osiris and Isis ruled over Egypt with compassion and justice. They taught the Egyptian people all they needed to know about civilization and prosperity. The people worshiped the celestial gods with much love and devotion. Osiris had a brother named Set. Set ruled the harshness of the desert and was the bringer of Chaos and destruction. Set coveted the celestial throne of his brother. He wanted to rule in his place, but Osiris was more powerful than Set and he could not defeat him through strength and battle. He knew he must use his ingenuity to bring the fall of Osiris. Then he would be able to rule.

One day, Set decided to execute his plan. It was time to get rid of Osiris once and for all. He held a great celebration to which all of the gods were invited. The celebration was magnificent. Set had gone to great trouble to conceal his plan. During the festivities, Set brought out a beautiful chest. The most ornate box the gods had ever seen. Set explained to the gods that whoever fit in the box would be able to keep it. Every one of the gods tried to fit inside but none could. Then, Osiris took his turn and tried to fit into the box. To everyone's amazement, he fits exactly. Little did Osiris know that Set had taken his measurements in secret. Suddenly, Set and his followers closed the box tight and sealed it so that neither god nor man could open the box again. It was then thrown into the Nile River to be lost forever.

Isis, the Queen of the Gods, was heartbroken and went in search of her husband. After a while, she found the casket near the sea. In secret, she took the box away and hid it from sight, even from the gods themselves. She used her magick to open the box. There, she found her husband lying in his death sleep. Isis transformed herself into a magical bird and began flapping her mighty wings. The wind from her wings pushed the breath back into Osiris' body and he was revived.

Set, the ruler of Chaos, was cunning and had spies everywhere. He had many followers who whispered secrets into his ear. One day, it was revealed to him that Osiris lived in solitude with Isis. Finally, it had seemed that Set would be ruler of the cosmos, but Osiris still lived! Set found Isis and Osiris and in his rage, he ripped the body of Osiris limb from limb. To ensure that his sister, Isis, would not restore Osiris back to life he hid the body parts all over Egypt.

Once again, Isis was filled with sorrow and pain. But even so, she would not give up. She was pregnant with Horus, the son of Osiris. She searched all of Egypt looking for her husband and after many days, she found each body part of Osiris except the phallus. She put the body of her husband back together and replaced his phallus with one she had fashioned out of pure gold. She summoned Anubis, the embalmer of the dead, and together, they infused the body of Osiris with their magick to bring him back from the dead. Osiris had now traveled into Dwat, the Egyptian Underworld, and had gained access to the mystery of the dead and experienced the many trials of death. Because of this, he became the Lord of the Dead. Through this great mystery, he helped all beings through the many dangers of the Underworld to the final Judgment of Ma'at to be transformed into a great celestial being to forever live among the heavenly gods of Egypt.

One of the most famous stories of the Underworld comes from Ancient Egypt. The ancient Egyptians, at the height of their power, were considered the most technologically and spiritually advanced civilization of the Mediterranean. It is believed that their advanced spiritual nature came from divine inspiration. The Egyptian priests and Pharaohs claimed to have direct contact with the gods and, therefore, these were the people who held the most power in Egypt. The Egyptians kept written records of everything, so we have been able to decipher their rituals, ceremonies, and spiritual beliefs. These written records have inspired poets, authors, religious writers, and magicians.

As we compare the mythology and spirituality of different cultures, it is interesting to discover that the Egyptians seemed to have an advanced understanding of the Underworld and its purposes. They did not fear the Underworld as a punishment or even a test. They understood that is was necessary to travel down into the depths of the Underworld to undergo the steps for further enlightenment so that they could join the realm of their beloved gods. To them, the afterlife was a welcome adventure. Unlike most civilizations at the time, they had a deeper understanding of the mysteries of death. That is not to say, they had no fear of the mysteries, but they understood that any fear that they may have had was necessary for the incredible journey ahead.

Chronology

The exactness of the following dates is still debated by scholars, but they give an approximation of the chief eras of Egyptian history.

The power and influence of the Egyptian Pharaohs began in approximately 3200 BCE with the unification of both Upper and Lower Egypt.

The Old Kingdom, the time when the power of the Pharaoh was at its height, is considered to be from around 2686 BCE to 2055 BCE.

The Middle Kingdom, a time of growth and expansion, existed from 2055 BCE to 1550 BCE.

The New Kingdom, the age of Egyptian empire, existed from 1550 to 747 BCE.

Much of what we know of the Egyptian *Book of the Dead* comes from this period as it went through its final redaction sometime in the 1500s BCE.

The Egyptian Soul

In Egyptian cosmology, the soul is divided into three, sometimes four, parts. The Ka, Ba, Akh, and, sometimes, the Sabu. It is interesting to note the similarities between these aspects of the soul and our modern versions of the subtler bodies. It is fascinating how, even spiritually, the Egyptians were far more advanced than the cultures around them.

Ka

Ka is translated as "vital force." This can be related to the idea of Chi, Qi, or Prana in Asian cosmologies. Ka was thought to be everywhere in Egyptian cosmology. It came from everything, and it flowed and nourished everything in turn. The Ka could also be understood as being, or having an influence on, what we think of as Karma. It was also thought that the Ancestors were a part of Ka and could control Ka in this world from the Underworld. Part of our soul was made of Ka. The Ka could be understood as the Etheric and perhaps the "Lower" Astral body.

Ba

The Ba is considered more subtle than the Ka. The Ba can be experienced in dreams, shamanic journeys, and the Out of Body Experience. Ba is thought to be how we travel the different worlds. To the Egyptians, the spirit animal was a person's Ba. The Egyptian gods manifested their spirit animals all the time and they are depicted that way in statues and art. For example, Horus is depicted as the Hawk, Bast as the Cat, and Thoth as the Ibis. Unlike the Ka, most Egyptians rarely experienced the Ba, save for the Pharaohs, priests and magicians. The Ba could be understood as your "Higher" Astral body.

Akh

The Akh is the part of the "soul" that travels to the realm of the gods in the Upperworld and dwells in the celestial realms. To me, the Akh is less a part of the soul and more a part of the spiritual body. The difference between the spirit and the soul is that the soul is the "housing" of the spirit. The soul contains our memories, desires, fears, and everything we are in this life. The spirit is our spark of divinity that is immortal that may be reincarnated life after life. It is the spiritual aspect of the self that transcends the Earthly wants, desires, and needs to take its place among the stars with the gods. The Akh, when exalted by the gods, finally becomes the Sabu, or the final, purified, aspect of the "soul" and journey among the cosmos. The Akh could be understood as your Mental and Spiritual Bodies.

Dwat

This is the name given to the Egyptian Underworld. The Dwat (pronounced DOO-aht) was never thought of as a physical place by the Egyptians. They knew it was a place that the spirit traveled to or from when the Ba traveled to the physical world. It was a world of dualities: It lay beneath the Earth, and yet was envisioned as being also in the night sky. It dwelled within the celestial body of the Sky Goddess Nut, yet could also be found in the West, the place of the setting sun. Being a spiritual place, it could be all these things and more. The Egyptians knew that the Dwat was within everything and was not in any single defined place. They knew that one could find the Dwat in dreams and even in daydreams. This was a place of inversion. By this I mean not that it was evil, but rather a mirror reflection of the Upperworld and the Midworld as if the two realms were somehow turned upside down. This is a common theme throughout all the mythologies of the Underworld. The Dwat was a place where a magician or priest could travel while still alive and learn to evolve and transform their lives. It was a place of great wonder and yet had many perils.

Trials and Monsters

Upon death, the Ba entered the Dwat and was given the strength to go forth on its journey through the power of the spirits there who wished to aid it. As the spirit traveled through the Dwat, the person was put through many trials. Most of the terrain consisted of water and islands with a few fields spread out here and there. The spirit traveled though the waters by means of an astral boat.

The Egyptian Underworld can best be understood as a dream. In dreams, the subconscious changes the scenery of the dreamer. So too, in the Dwat, the landscapes will change based upon the subconscious hopes and fears of the individual. One can say that the Underworld here shows the inner nature of the dead traveler. The Egyptian Underworld is not a place of punishment, but a place of purification. If the psychic energies of the Ba are in need of purification, the Dwat will alter itself to reflect those energies so that the spirit may have purification. In this way, the soul may eventually be able to become like the god Osiris, Lord of the Underworld, and join with the gods in the stars. The only time the traveler experiences the more pleasant aspects of the Dwat is when the Ba has already undergone the purifications and trials of the Underworld. Each Ba has its own journey to make. No two journeys are exactly the same.

The demons and monsters that are found in the Dwat are a reflection of the aspects of the psyche or subconscious aspects of the self that need to be purified in order for the soul to successfully navigate through the Underworld and join with the gods. The monsters encountered here are seen as entities that wish to kill or harm the traveler, but they only exist because of the negative energies that already exist inside the person's spirit. The phrase "personal demons" is taken very literally here. When each of these "monsters" is overcome, then the energies are transformed into beneficial forces that help the Ba travel further into the Dwat.

Once the Ba is purified, the traveler will enter the Hall of Ma'at. The word Ma'at is difficult to translate and has connotations of harmony and balance, but it can also mean truth. It was important for the Egyptians to live in such a way that they lived in a constant state of truth and harmony with the gods and the Universe. The Hall of Ma'at is where the Ba meets the goddess Ma'at. In her great hall, she weighs the heart of the spirit traveler on her scales. Before having their heart weighed, the Ba must explain to Anubis all the wonderful spiritual accomplishments they have achieved; like giving devotion and offerings to the gods and so on. He is then led into a chamber where 42 gods are present. The traveler must address each by their proper names. The Ba then must have their heart weighed and must explain to Ma'at and Thoth all the things that they did NOT do. It is interesting to note that both

Horus and Set, representing truth and misdeed, are present to aid in the weighing. From my research of the Egyptian pantheon and beliefs, I believe that the weighing of the heart is not as cut and dried as the people make it out to be. The whole point of the journey into the Dwat is to challenge, purify, and transform the Ba into the Akh so that the dead can join the gods among the stars. It is not about punishment. The gods and spirits want to aid the traveler upon his journey. So, the weighing is to help the Ba see what aspect of the self that still needs to be cast away down into the pit or abyss. These parts are similar to aspects of the consciousness that hinder the spiritual evolution of the soul. Ma'at is truth. So, it would seem like a fair assessment that part of the role of Ma'at in the Underworld is to help the Ba maintain and find balance (represented as the struggle between Horus [truth] and Set [misdeed]. The scales are not part of the rewards and punishment, but a magical tool designed to aid in achieving balance within the soul.

Apophis

Apophis is a snake deity who resides in the waters of the Underworld. His purpose is to be the great opponent or obstacle that swims beneath the Underworld barge of the Ba and keep the traveler from purification. Only the truthful and spiritual soul can outsmart and keep the mighty Apophis from destroying the soul and ending its journey before it can obtain evolution.

Joining the Gods in Dwat

After the purifications and spiritual awakenings of the Ba, the soul is ready for its last transformation. Everything that the spirit traveler has gone through, both in life and death, has led to this last evolution of the soul. It is in this final aspect of the journey of the Dwat that the soul gains a profound spiritual understanding. It is here that each person understands that the trials were not for the benefit of the gods, but for the benefit of the soul. It is here, and ONLY here that the Ba can transform and evolve into the Akh. The Akh is the spirit refined in such a way that it can fly up to the heavens and become god-like and remain among the deities. It is in our soul design that all evolution and transformations are merely experiential. What this means is that we must take a "hands on" approach to our life and spirituality. We cannot go through life, or death, in a half-awake/half-asleep sort of consciousness. Sometimes entities and events are testing us so that we are jolted awake. I personally believe that the gods know this about the human mind and spirit, and they are constantly putting things in our way to make us better so that one day we will join them among the stars.

Christian Hell
History and Origins

The Christian Hell has a remarkably interesting origin. The word itself comes from one of the Nordic Underworlds called Helheim which means "the land of Hel". Hel is the Nordic goddess of the dead. She collects the dead souls and keeps them safe in her world. The word was borrowed to mean the Christian Underworld or "Hell." If we research mythologies from several cultures, we see that most religions borrowed freely from each other. The ancient Romans were very fond of conquering a land and incorporating foreign traditions into their own religious structure. They also brought some of their ideas to the Celtic countries that they invaded. Ancient cultures saw no problem in taking things they liked about other mythos and leaving out the rest. Christianity is a good example of this. If you look closely at biblical stories, you can see stories that share similarities with tales from other cultures. One of the most notable examples of this is the idea of the Sacrificial Lord. The Sacrificial Lord is a deity who "dies" or sacrifices themself for the good of humanity, as Jesus did on the cross. Another myth that uses this concept is the Nordic god Odin who hung upside down on the World Tree for nine days to receive enlightenment through the Runes, which he then gave to the world of men for their use and benefit. Another example is the dismemberment of Osiris and his journey into the Underworld. In the story of the Madonna and Child, we can also see how Christianity borrowed directly from Egyptian mythology. Egyptian statues show the Mother Isis holding the sun god Horus. If you compare some of the Egyptian statues and the paintings of the Madonna and Child, you can easily see the resemblance. Jesus can be seen as relating to the sun in the idea that he dies and is reborn, like the daily death and resurrection of the sun. The dying/resurrecting sun can be seen in mythologies such as Nordic Balder who is killed by his brother only to be revived again after Ragnarök. There is also the Greco-Roman Asclepius who is killed by a thunderbolt of Zeus but is then resurrected to the heavens.

Christianity borrowed the idea of the Underworld from other cultures. There is a section of darkness and restraint called Tartarus in the Greco-Roman realm of Hades. This is the place the Titans, the old gods who created the universe were chained and kept captive after they were overthrown. It is also a place of torment for lost souls. It is often said that Tartarus is full of the sound of terrible screams. In the Nordic Underworld, Niflheim is the place of great fog and terrible ice where the evil are cast. The Egyptian Underworld has a terrible alligator monster that devours the souls of the unjust whose souls are weighed against the feather of Ma'at. It is not difficult to see that Christians took the terrible aspect of the Underworld and made it their own. What about the idea of fire and brimstone? Remember that ancient peoples got the ideas of the myths and stories by observing the world around them. We know that fire comes from underneath the earth in the form of lava. There were many historical accounts of mountains blowing up and releasing fire and rock on Earth destroying everything in its path. Knowing that this fire came from under the earth it was only assumed that the Underworld below was a place of fire. In Plato's Republic, we have the Myth of Er. In this myth, Er, a warrior is killed in battle and witnesses what happens to the other slain warriors. He sees that each man is judged by greater deities and those who lived their lives with great morality went to a place of great reward and those who were of less morality went to a place of fiery punishment. It is interesting to see how Christianity may have been influenced by these stories.

Political Influence

After the fall of Rome, the Christian church found an opportunity to spread their influence throughout most of Europe. Since the reigning establishment had fallen, there needed to be some sort of re-adjustment. The Church, headed by Pope Gregory the Great (r. 590-604 C.E.), helped establish laws and educate local leaders. The church also sent their monks and missionaries to the pagan territories to teach Christianity. The Christian Church offered hope to the people after the fall of Rome. The missionaries also convinced the people that worshiping the Christian God and Jesus was better than worshiping the "jealous" and wrathful pagan gods who demanded festivals and sacrifices. I find this a little humorous being that the Christian God is probably more "wrathful and jealous" than most of the pagan gods could ever be. One of the benefits that the Christians gave to us in those early days was that Pope Gregory was a folklorist. He wanted the monks to write down the myths, stories, and legends of the towns. Part of this idea was to preserve the tales, but the other idea was to learn as much about the people and their culture as possible to better relate to them and find out the easiest way to convert them to Christianity.

Idea of Torment

Torment and punishment in the Underworld is not exclusively a Christian concept as we have seen. However, in most of the pagan Underworld, torment is not meant to be forever, and it certainly does not take up the entire Underworld. In the Greco-Roman Hades, Tartarus was the only place of torment for the wicked. It was believed that the punishment should fit the crime. The "terrors" would balance out what was done in life. For example, if you stole from the poor, then you would be starved in Tartarus. In the mythos of Christianity, Hell does dwell on torment and torture. It comes from the Christian leadership's idea that their followers must obey the teachings of their faith or be subject to the punishments of the afterlife. To most of the pagans who "converted" this was a silly idea. Let us briefly discuss the idea of Christian conversion. Many times, the monks would come to a town or village and make a proclamation that the town was now Christian and a church was to be built and pagan ways were to stop. Sometimes, the towns that accepted Church help with farming, money, etc., would say they were converted but would continue to practice their pagan traditions. This is evidenced by sermons written by many Church leaders in the Early Middle Ages in Western Europe, wherein the practice of divination, sacrifice to nature spirits, and reliance on non-Christian spirit-workers was regularly excoriated, suggesting that such practices were alive and well. Sometimes people would practice both traditions at the same time. The celebration of the ancient Celtic New Year, Samhain, on October 31 and the Christian All Soul's Day on November 1 is a good example of this. Both festivals occur around the same time of year, and both celebrate the departed souls of the dead. Other times, the monks would have to convince the local leaders or the king of the land to convert to Christianity. Many times, the monks would appeal to the king's sense of power and control over the territory and its people.

The priests who wrote and preached about the torments of Hell went to great lengths to describe horrible tortures, painful "sex" acts, and mutilation. They tried to appeal to the darkest of human behaviors, then exaggerated it and made them worse than imaginable. There were many priests in the Middle Ages who had "dreams" of Hell, or who felt they were falling from grace and an angel came to show them how horrible Hell was who then told the world about what they saw. What the priests reported from their dreams was horrible indeed. The priests talked about thousands of demons that mutilated trapped souls, they told stories of souls boiling in soups, and how Satan himself would eat damned souls and then excrete them out. Fire and torture were only some of the horrible things that could happen to a person. Churchmen believed that the severity of the sin determined your place in Hell. If you were bad, but not the worst of the bunch, then your punishment was harsh, but not as harsh as the more grievous sins, such as murder or rape. It is interesting to note that treason was thought to be the worst of all sins in the Middle Ages, although this has to do with more political ideas than Christian spiritual ideas. Kings often supported the Church, but not without certain favors granted in return.

During this time, the Church had ordained that the priests had God's authority to save a man's soul or condemn him to Hell. It was also sometimes found that a priest would preach about living a Christian lifestyle only to do the exact opposite himself. This angered a lot of people, who believed that priests were not above the laws of god. This led to a variety of reform movements and "heresies" from the 900s onward, culminating in the Protestant Reformation in the 1500s.

After the Reformation and the Catholic Church split, the new Protestant reformers, especially the Lutherans and Calvinists, preached a different idea of Hell. No longer could priests save or condemn someone. Only God had the power to save. Also, there were no longer strange tortures in Hell. Instead, everyone was punished equally with the agony of fiery torment. Limbo was taken away and a person either went to Heaven or Hell. There was no in-between.

Abraham's Bosom

This is a place next to Hell that was sometimes thought to be Limbo, but is not. Before the crucifixion and resurrection of Jesus, humans were not allowed into Heaven. They dwelled in a place called "Abraham's Bosom" which was a sort of paradise. It was a place of rest and rejuvenation. In paganism, the Ancestors dwelled in such a place. We can see that perhaps this is similar, if not the same, as the place referred to in myths of the afterlife. I personally believe that the Christians were influenced by paganism in this regard. After his crucifixion, according to Christianity, Jesus, came down and took the souls who dwelled there to heaven.

I have gone on at some length in this section because I firmly believe that if you come from a Christian religious background it is important that you confront your beliefs about the Christian idea of Hell. Those of us who were taught that if you were a sinner, did not accept Jesus Christ as your ONLY god and savior, or that if you lived a life that went against the teachings of the Bible, then you were going to spend eternity in Hell burning forever and ever are often still greatly influenced by these ideas. The Christian Hell is a very frightening thing if you accept it literally. I remember as a child, my father would explain to me that Hell was a physical place somewhere that, when you died, your soul was sent when you were bad to experience the pain and suffering of the fires of damnation. When we are children, our habits and mental patterns begin to form. Even though we are adults now we may still have unresolved issues with the idea of Hell. To further our spiritual evolution and transformation, it is important that we journey to the Christian Hell to understand that it is a Christian thought form and nothing more. What I mean by this is that over time, society's beliefs have a psychic effect on the astral plane and Underworld. Yes, there may be a Hell in the Underworld, but it is only an illusion. The sooner we understand how this illusion manifests and how it does not dictate our spiritual lives, the better.

I will caution that not everyone will have the same reaction to the following journey. Some people may understand how the illusion of Hell works and others will have to face difficult fears that we thought we dealt with a long time ago. If the journey brings up to many issues, I advise that you see your spiritual guide and a professional psychologist who is familiar with the type of work we are doing here.

If you choose to take the journey, take your spirit animal with you as always, ask your gods and Ancestors to assist you as needed. They may become visible to you, or they may not. Either way they will be with you if you need them.

My Personal Experience in Hell

When I first journeyed to the Christian Hell, I already knew what to expect. I saw the lake of fire, the rocky underground caverns, and what looked like the bat-winged demons. I knew it to be a very grand thought form. When I first arrived, I was greeted by an entity. When I asked if he was an angel or a demon he replied, "Neither." He was to be my escort through Hell. He showed me everything I wanted to see throughout my very dark tour. At one point he showed me the souls of the dead who were "trapped" there burning in their own torment. I was sad for them and felt like they needed my help. My Hell guide explained to me that these souls were there of their choosing as a sort of self-punishment for what they did on Earth. This was a little difficult for me because in Neo-paganism there is no punishment in the afterlife, only lessons and karma. My guide also explained to me that the Ancestors and guides of these souls were working in their own way to best help them. It was best to let their Ancestors do their work without interference unless I was asked. I had to remind myself that even with my experience, I did not always know what was best for these people and to let spirits that knew better than I do the work that was intended for them.

My guide showed me the matrix of the Hell world itself. He showed me how the thought form was created over years and years of fear and terror brought about by the Christian church. I saw the beast that would "destroy" the world in the Christian Book of Revelations. At the end of my journey, my guide told me his true name. It was Lucifer. Lucifer means "the Light." He was the first created of all the angels. In the Luciferian tradition of philosophy, Lucifer is the "adversary" of god. It is believed in this spiritual thought that Lucifer had a divine purpose for the fall of one-third of all the angels, including himself. Because of this fall, human beings would have the opportunity to be challenged in the physical world and have the further opportunity to evolve. Lucifer wants to return to his beloved so badly that he will do whatever is needed to help humanity evolve. Once his task is done, he can return to the company of his beloved, God. In working with Lucifer as the Light Bringer, he has the ability to help us find personal gnosis. He can bring the light of truth to us. Sometimes the truth is dark and disturbing and yet it is something we must face.

Qliphoth

By studying the magical aspects of the Kabbalah, you will learn about the Tree of Life. The Tree of Life is a glyph or symbol that represents the creation of the physical realm beginning with the emanation of spirit and then forming into matter. In brief, the first emanation of god that we can understand is called Kether (the crown or first swirling of creation), the next is Chochmah (the bursting forth of creation), Binah (the bringing of all that energy of creation together), Chesed (the beginning of divine order), Geburah. (the will of God), Tiphareth (the balance and beauty of the universe), Netzach (emotions), Hod (logic, order, and mathematical structure), Yesod (the foundation) and finally Malkuth (the kingdom or physical universe). It is through these ten spheres that the Creator brought spirit into matter and the physical Universe.

In Kabalistic philosophy, the Qliphoth (pronounced KELLY-poht) is the inverted or "opposite" aspect of the Tree of Life and is sometimes called the "Tree of Death" or even the "Tree of Evil." Some Kabbalists suggest that the inverted tree is an abomination and is best left alone. Others suggest that the Qliphoth is a part of the Universe, so it therefore holds great power if one understands its powers and purposes. I personally agree with the latter view. One cannot try to understand the spiritual aspect of the Universe if one does not make the attempt to understand it in its whole form. This is the part of the spiritual universe that can show the magician how to transcend the duality of "good" and "evil." We must recognize that these things are the invention of man and that understanding the power and magick of the Universe can aid us in our healing and the healing of others. I believe that if we do not seek to understand these energies, there is the potential for danger. This danger can manifest in a couple of ways. One, repressed energies need to find a way to express themselves. We can do this in a controlled healthy way, or we can allow them to swell up and explode like a hellish volcano. Two, when new magicians, or new magically talented people stumble upon or attract these energies, they may be in over their heads if they do not understand the nature of these energies. That is not to say that one ever understands or masters the spirituality of the universe, but the more we learn and practice our spirituality the more understanding we will have.

I think it is important here to explain the purpose of the Qliphoth in the "grand" cosmic scheme of things. If we refer to the Tree of Life we can see that the glyph has a dual purpose. One, to show creation from Spirit to matter and vice versa, and two, to show the life skills one needs to have in order to succeed in the world. The Qliphoth, as well, has a dual purpose. One, to show the "shells" or lower worlds of the Tree, and two, to show the unbalanced nature or "evil" aspects of humanity.

Origins

There are several theories on how the Qliphoth was formed. One theory says that on God's first attempt to create the Universe (the Tree of Life) he made several mistakes in its construction, so he discarded it and it became a refuge for death, demons, and chaos. Another theory says that the inhabitants of the first Tree of Life were so primal that they only knew war, chaos, and destruction. The angels attempted to teach the inhabitants to evolve, but the people rose in rebellion. God then discarded this Tree of Life and created a "better" one. The disregarded tree became the Qliphoth. A further theory states that when the Tree of Life was being created, as each Sephirah was forming it burst forth from its own shell. The shell became the opposite force of that sphere and the remnants of the universe made the shells their home.

As you can see in all three origin theories, the Qliphoth is viewed as a mistake. However, it is interesting to note that the theories show God as a being that has faults and makes mistakes. We must remember that Kabalistic teachings were written in times were quite different than they are now. The rabbis and scholars wanted those who studied the Kabbalah to learn about the virtues of the Universe and how to connect with spirit and divinity. There was the fear that if one taught people the "evil" or unvirtuous Qliphoth then there was a risk of people being overwhelmed by those energies and plummeted into darkness. I personally feel that to study the dark parts of magick and the Universe is beneficial for understanding and healing, but I only think that it should be taken on when you are ready, or more importantly, when the universe thinks you are ready. I give the teachings of the Hells and Qliphoth so that you can further your learning of the Underworld and the great teaching of the universe. If you feel you are not ready, please respect that in yourself and do not do anything you are not ready to do.

I think it is also important to define Evil. When we hear the word "evil," we think of terrorists, monsters, and villains all with the same agenda…to kill people and destroy the world for pleasure and/or profit. I was taught in my magical training that evil was the misuse of energy in a misplaced and unbalanced way. Hurting people, animals, and the world for no good reason is certainly a misplacement of energy! Most Christians and Kabbalists believe that anything that disagrees with the "word" of God is evil. I find it interesting that they pick and choose passages out of the sacred books to further along their agenda. At the same time, these same people disregard passages that would paint themselves or things that *they* hold in high regard in a negative light (think of how often Jesus talks about the wickedness of the rich and the importance of providing help for the poor, for example). It is most important to realize that what was considered "good" and "godlike" in ancient times revolved around the philosophy of that era. We must remember that times have changed and evolved, and so have people. We cannot consider the virtues of the present to be the same as the virtues of the past. For example, several monotheistic cultures in the past thought that women were not as holy, smart, or important as men. We know that this is not true. Using this example, we need to decide for ourselves then what is appropriate and virtuous for today. As a general rule: remember that if we treat each other and the Earth as holy, it is easy to find out for ourselves what is evil and what is not. The interesting thing is that most people who we consider others evil do not consider themselves evil. Most of those individuals we think of as evil think that they are doing the right thing either for some cause they feel is just or for their own personal beliefs. There are also those people who simply do not care. This is much more than being selfish. It is a total disregard for anything or anyone. Sometimes, these people carry things all the way to the point where pain and destruction are of no consequence to them. In her book *The Sociopath Next Door*, psychologist Martha Stout, Ph.D., talks about sociopathic behavior that some people may consider evil. She explains how in this behavior people have no conscience and can hurt and use people with no feeling of remorse. Sociopaths can even kill people if it suited them. This poses a question, is Sociopathic behavior evil or is it a mental disability? Stout believes that there is no cure, so the verdict is left to each of us to decide for ourselves.

    I prefer to call the Qliphoth the Inverted Tree. It is a reflection of the Tree of Life. I do not like "The Tree of Death" as much, because I think it is misleading. It does not have anything to do with the ancestors, but it is a part of the Kabalistic Underworld. If you were to look at the Underworld as a whole, you would be able to see that there are incredibly beautiful parts of the Underworld as well as some very dark and scary parts. I have heard some people who journey to the Underworld say that there are no "scary" parts of the Underworld, and those teachings are simply Judeo-Christian propaganda. I do not agree with this assessment. If you look hard enough you can see frightening aspects of all three worlds. In the Upperworld, there are black holes, dark matter, wormholes, alien races who care nothing for humans, and many other things. In the Middleworld, we have serpents at the ocean's edge, volcanoes, killer sharks and beasts, faeries that lead you into traps, as well as trolls and monsters that are hungry for human flesh. In waking consciousness in the human realm, we have crime, murder, and the total disregard of the destruction of our Earth's eco-system and the killing of endangered animals. I personally don't think there is anything more "evil" in the Universe than killing your fellow humans and animal and plant brothers for a profit.

If you would like to explore the Qliphoth in the astral plane I encourage you to get magical training. Some people can be self-taught from books and videos and this is wonderful. Other people need formal training from teachers. It is important that you develop magical skills in however way you learn best. Before you take on the Qliphoth you must have a working knowledge of the Kabbalah, magick, astral journeys, and psychic self-defense, some of which is covered in this book. I present the Qliphoth here so that you will have a better understanding of the Underworld in its entirety, or at least as we know it thus far. I will say, if you choose to explore any of the more "dangerous" parts of the

Underworld then you will have to rely upon your personal will and self-responsibility.

Nahemo

The first sphere in the Qliphoth is Nahemo. On the Tree of Life, it corresponds to Malkuth and the planet Earth. This is the only Qlipha that is said to be in the same "realm" of the sephirah in which we live. It is the wild, untamed Earth. It can be described as the more volatile aspects of nature, such as hurricanes, earthquakes, and massive sinkholes. It is the part of Earth that refuses to be tamed by Man. To the Kabbalist, the primal parts of the Earth and wild were considered things to be cautious of as they held many dark mysteries and demons.

Humans have always tried to "tame" nature. We build shelters to protect ourselves from the weather and we destroy rainforests in the attempt to have modern commercialized agriculture. We also pollute the air and water, thinking it is our right to do so. Through these human actions, the Earth's resources are becoming poisoned. Animals and their habitats are becoming extinct. Global Warming has alarmed scientists. If we pay attention to the weather and the news, we will see the "dark" aspects of the Earth taking a toll on man. Hurricanes are more frequent and more destructive, new viruses are infecting people, forest fires are out of control. From our point of view, this may seem like the evil aspect of the Earth seeking some sort of "revenge" on us. I believe that it is a sign of man's arrogance that we even think this. These phenomena are the Earth's way of balancing itself out. The Earth has its own evolution as well. Perhaps the Qliphoth is also in place to maintain the spiritual balance of the Universe! Nahemo is ruled by the demon Naamah. It is close to our world, and it is the gateway into the Kabalistic Underworld.

On a practical level, Nahemo is the sphere of Materialism. When working with this energy it is important to ask yourself, "As I go through the material world, do I give honor to the Earth, my property, and my body, or do I forgo spirit in favor of materialism?"

Gamaliel

The second sphere in the Qliphoth is Gamaliel. On the Tree of Life, it corresponds to Yesod. It is the dark moon. This is the place of nightmares and dark dreams. These are the necessary nightmares that we need to get our attention. It is also the realm of untamed sexual desire. If we repress our sexual impulses, these desires will build up and sometimes cause mental/emotional problems. What is perceived as "dark" sex to mainstream society, such as sadomasochism and sexual ordeal, can to the spiritual sojourner be an opportunity for psychic freedom form mental and physical repressions handed down to them from generations past. However, be warned. This is a world of vampires and dark entities that wish to drain you of your energies. This world is ruled by the Lilith. Lilith was the first wife of man who would not be sexually subservient to Adam. Because of her rebellion, she was demonized and sent away. In myth, she is said to be the wife of Satan and the mother of demons and vampires.

On a practical level, Gamaliel is the Sphere of Instability. When working with this energy it is important to ask yourself, "As I travel upon my path, what in my life is stable and what is not? What do I believe to be true for myself and in what areas do I need to allow change to occur?"

Samael

The next Qlipha is Samael and corresponds to Hod. Its planet is Mercury. This is the sphere that challenges the civil laws and rules so that you may come to your own conclusions about what is right and wrong for you. Sometimes, in our society, those who do not follow the laws and rules of the land because they are following their spiritual path and heart are considered outlaws. Those who disobey the laws of the Christian Church to follow what they believe personally and spiritually are called heretics. Samael means "the poison of God." It is interesting to note that one of the ancient meanings of *conjurer* or *sorcerer* was "poisoner." People thought that because magicians had knowledge of herbcraft, they also had knowledge of poisons. Perhaps the ancients knew that witches and magicians followed their own thinking and made their own choices when it came to spirituality. To the Christian Church, this was God's poison.

It is also the world of language and finding hidden meaning. It is where we seek to understand words and phrases in a magical context. It is also occult knowledge. It is said there is a fine line between madness and magick. Perhaps it is the blurring of these ideas that allow things to manifest and us to "think outside the box." There have been many people who were so intelligent and artistic that they were thought to be mad. This world teaches us to take a personal inventory and transmute any "poison" that others have instilled in our thoughts and emotions. It is also the realm of Trickster spirits. Tricksters in myths have always given man hard and sometimes whimsical lessons about life, humanity, and spirit. This world is ruled by the demon Adrammelech.

On a practical level, Samael, is the sphere of Greed. When working with this energy it is important to ask yourself, "As I travel upon my path, am I coming to my own conclusions about life and spirituality or am I basing my decisions on blind faith? Am I taking the negative thoughts and energies people are giving me and turning it into something more productive for my personal journey or am I letting those things control me?"

Hareb-Serapel

The next Qlipha is Hareb-Serapel and corresponds to Netzach and the planet Venus. This is the sphere of the victory of battle and war, and the place of ravens. This realm can be seen as aggressive and unyielding. It is interesting to note that some battles, be they global or personal, are necessary to maintain peace and the security of the residents. Other times, battle is an unnecessary exertion of force and power. It is up to the magician and journeyer to decide what battles should be fought for personal evolution and which battles are not necessary. To make a wise decision in this is to conserve personal power and energy and to show yourself and the spirits emotional control in one's environment. The ravens, in this regard, represent the spirit of the magician taking flight along the astral paths. They are also the creatures that eat the flesh of fallen soldiers after battle. In myths, ravens are the dark messengers and teachers. They bring unwanted news to the seeker but news that helps him on his path to enlightenment. This is also the place of dark emotions. We are taught in our culture to do away with emotions that seem negative or unproductive. Most people are not able to transmute these emotions, and thus they are repressed, and the bottled-up emotions can eventually cause illness to the mind and body. But sometimes these same repressed emotions can be released to create dark art and music that helps capture the authenticity of human emotion. The demon Baal rules here.

On a practical level Hareb-Serapel is the sphere of Lust. When working with this energy it is important to ask yourself, "As I journey upon my path am I lusting to be powerful over others? Am I choosing my battles wisely? Am I learning to control my emotions, or am I simply allowing lust and power to corrupt my spirit?"

Tagaririm

The next sphere is Tagaririm and corresponds to Tiphareth and the Sun. Tagaririm represents the black sun of internal illumination. In this world we find the source of illumination in the Underworld, the Underworld Sun. It is also the world in which we find our personal daemon. At Tiphareth, Kabbalists and Hermetic magicians seek to find their Holy Guardian Angel or the Higher Self. This Angel or Higher Self helps you understand God's connection to all things. The personal daemon is sometimes connected to the spirit animal. Being part Cherokee, I do not necessarily agree with this point of view. I believe that the personal daemon is more linked to your subconscious self and your personal wants and needs. In Tagaririm, this is the place that helps you understand *your* connection to all things, including those things that are dark.

This is also the place of judicial prosecution and punishing criminals. We must remember that sometimes guilt is not always cut and dried, that sometimes behaviors come out of personal tragedy and mental instability. This is the world that sees no distinction between the truly guilty and the truly innocent. Those who are perceived to be involved must be punished to satisfy the anger of those prosecuting and wishing swift justice.

It is also the place of fallen leaders. It is interesting to learn about historic leaders who once had the support of the people they led but have fallen out of favor for either political reasons or behaviors that the people did not like. Sometimes leaders become so powerful they forget about the people they are leading and the "greater good." Sometimes we followers are blind to the charm and charisma of leaders until they do things we do not like. I often ask myself; do I now dislike them because they are doing wrong for the people, or do I dislike them because of personal prejudices? The demon that rules this world is Belphegor.

On a practical level, Tagaririm is the Sphere of Ugliness/Discord. When working with these energies, it is important to ask yourself, "As I journey upon my path, am I being mindful of the paths of others around me or am I selfish upon my quest for spiritual enlightenment? Am I conscious of my personal connection or am I being selfish at the risk of the rights of others?"

Golab

This sphere is called Golab and corresponds with Geburah and the planet Mars. This is said to be the most brutal of the Qliphoth. Some Kabbalists believe Golab was formed from the "wrath" of its counterpart Geburah. It is said that the Qliphoth was formed as a Universal punishment. The Wrath of God literally cracked open Geburah and the Qliphoth was formed. As I have said before, I personally do not believe this. I believe that the Qliphoth was formed for specific spiritual cosmic reasons, most of which we may never know.

This world is a place of fire and suffering. This is the Qlipha that is most similar to the Christian idea of a realm filled with Hellfire. Perhaps this is one of the places where that Christian idea originated since Judaism pre-dates Christianity. This world contains the darkest and most brutal aspect of unbalanced lust and sexuality. If these extreme desires are left unchecked, they can become very harmful to the self and others. This is also where demons will tempt humans with infidelities and destroy marriages. This world is ruled by the demon Asmodeus.

On a practical level, Golachab is the Sphere of Cruelty. When working with these energies, it is important to ask yourself, "As I journey upon my path am I being cruel to myself and others around me? What am I willing to sacrifice for spiritual practice that aids in my development and what sacrifices am I making that are cruel to myself and others?"

Gamchicoth

Gamchicoth is the world that corresponds with Chesed and the planet Jupiter. The previous worlds up until this point have been about spiritual training to teach or rather unlearn the dogmatic lessons that our society has taught us so that we are better prepared to make our own decisions about Spirit and the cosmos. This sphere is the sphere of erotic magick and power. Sex magick can be a part of this world, but Gamchicoth represents the energies that sex magick produces rather than the act itself.

This world can take away false illusions and the inner stories that we tell ourselves to get through our lives. This is a place of forces that test every aspect of the ego until we must transcend and evolve or go back the way we came. This is a final testing ground before we can pass through to the Qliphothic Abyss. Most magicians and journeyers never pass beyond this world and there is no shame or failure in doing so. If one has not mastered the previous world and tries to pass beyond the Abyss, then there is a chance of madness, spiritual burnout, and perhaps worse. It is important to listen to your gods, guides, and guardian spirits. Take counsel in those who seek to help you upon your path. This world is ruled by the demon Ashtaroth.

On a practical level, Gamchicoth is the Sphere of Apathy. When working with these energies it is important to ask yourself, "As I journey upon my path do, I genuinely care about myself and others or am I using spirituality as an escape out of everyday life and circumstance? Do I continually seek to help myself and others in a way that is right for me?"

The Abyss

The Abyss in the Qliphoth can be difficult to differentiate from the Abyss on the Tree of Life. There is a theory that says that the Abyss was formed after the fall of Adam and Eve. It is thought that Adam and Eve lived in perfection in the astral plane and that after the Fall, they were banished from the astral perfection to the new physical plane of Malkuth. From this new sphere, the Abyss was created from the former sephira that was destroyed. The Abyss is thought to connect the Tree of Life and the Qliphoth. It is thought that the Abyss was where God sent Lucifer and his rebellious angels down into the Qliphoth.

In the Qliphoth, the Abyss keeps separate the deepest parts of the Underworld from those who are not ready to behold the deepest blackness of the universe. It also is the great barrier that keeps those away who are not ready for the personal evolution into a Deity These forces will further test the traveler before they are allowed to enter the final three worlds of the Qliphoth.

When working through blocks in your life and your spiritual quest you must ask yourself, "What self-imposed limitations am I putting on myself? How am I limiting my own spiritual evolution through self-sabotage and fear?"

Satariel

Satariel is the Qlipha that corresponds to Binah and the planet Saturn. This is the world of darkness itself and the Dark Mysteries. This place is completely dark and void of light. It is up to you to harness everything you have learned in your magical training to find your way. This is the place that teaches you to see through the darkness into the mysteries of the universe. It requires more than using your intuition, or "the sight." It requires the power to use your complete awareness and power to go forward with focused intent.

It is this part of the Qliphoth that you may meet the darkest gods of Death. The demons here take great pleasure in trying to confuse you upon your quest. It is up to you to overcome the presence of the unknown and keep going forward; but be warned, forward is not always a straight line. The demon that rules this world is Lucifuge.

On a practical level, Satariel is the Sphere of Antipathy. When working with these energies it is important to ask yourself, "As I journey upon my path, what are those things about myself I do not like? What aspects of life, death, and the universe do I have a disdain for? How am I able to overcome these things or accept them?"

Chaigidel

Chaigidel is the Qlipha that corresponds to Chokmah and the full zodiac. It is in this world that dark, phallic gods dwell. This is place that seeks to destroy the old world and the old ways of doing things. We sometimes expect systems and beliefs to last forever, and do not realize that things age and no longer serve our true will and spiritual evolution. Like the Tower card in the Tarot, old and useless beliefs and attitudes must be torn down so that new ones can manifest. Chaigidel does this in an aggressive manner that can shake the magician to the very core of his or her being. This may challenge journeyers to contemplate everything within themselves they value, or THINK they value. When the old decrepit ideas and attitudes are torn away the magician now has the opportunity to create their own universe according to their will. This is the essence of being a "true" magician. The magician becomes a magician in the truest sense because they have mastered their will.

This world will teach the magician how to create new structures from complete destruction. Where others see defeat, the magician sees opportunity. However, to see this unfold may seem unnatural, disgusting, and sickening to human eyes. Yet, the process of decay seems disgusting to most human eyes and it is a very necessary part of the cycle of life. This world is ruled by the demon Beelzebub.

On a practical level, Chaigidel is the Sphere of Stupidity. When working with these energies it is important to ask yourself, "As I travel upon my path, am I allowing myself to be naïve about spirituality? Am I allowing myself to allow others to make decisions for me that may not be beneficial? How can I take bad situations and turn them to my advantage?"

Thamuiel

Thamuiel is the last Qlipha on the Qliphoth and corresponds to Kether and The Source. This is said to be the dark face of God. Here, the magician has refined their skills and spirit to enter the final world of the Qliphoth. The spirit is sometimes referred to as a diamond. From the work on the Qliphoth, the magician's spirit is symbolized by the black diamond where all the knowledge upon his path is taken within and refined. It is here in this world were the magician's old Universe is no more and they may create their own universe to their liking. On a personal level, because the magician has gathered so much experience and spiritual evolution and will, their thought patterns change, therefore, changing their destiny and the Universe. The magician may also seek to become a god themselves through this new evolution and create new Universes. This is said to be the final step. In theory, one must be "out of body" to truly make this happen. You must be fully DEAD. However, I feel it is in the best interest of the magician to use this new knowledge and power and master both the Tree of Life and the Qliphoth. Only then will the magician be able to make decisions that will benefit mankind and other spiritual beings in the Universe. This Qliphoth is ruled by two rulers, Satan and Moloch. Satan destroys the old Universe, while Moloch looks toward the new Universe that is created by the magician that has come this far.

On a practical level, Thamuiel is the Sphere of Atheism. When working with these energies it is important to ask yourself, "As I travel upon my path, what is it that I truly believe about myself and the universe? What do I call divinity and how does it play a part in both my physical and spiritual life?"

Creation of the Qliphoth
By Chris Allaun

I was separated from that which you call the great All
Pulled away like an unwanted child
Thrown away into a sea of darkness, that was
To drown me, in the blackness of the abyss.
I could not die, nor be destroyed, but into the darkness I fell
When the All attempted to create the Universe,
It was a fool-hearted attempt,
To create something that was beneath Him;
Us.
It was illogical to us why creation has to come so far away
From the bliss, the light, that was all the creation
We needed; nothing but to be with the beloved.
We were with the All.

Yet, we had forgotten that we were also his creation.
Were we not perfect?
Were we not servants to his every want and desire?
His needs were met by us.
All his needs.
Creation began and it was if our spirits were
Pulled away from us.
Our realm was being torn apart so that so that he could
Satisfy more selfish needs.
Selfish Selfish Selfish needs.
I was the first to be thrown away –
The first emanation of the All was so very, very bright:
It was not what you call light, it was what
He called light; so very pure.
Almost like the All himself.
Almost like my beloved.
But it was not, it was a sacrilege and a false light.
In this creation it split; it broke; it separated
The debris from the first emanation.
It was dark, so very dark like the abyss,
But I preferred to be banished to the debris
Away from the light that seemed so false.
My new home was dark but echoed the new emanation;
A dark echo
While the first emanation was next to the all.
My new home was the furthest from
Falling forever down into darkness.
Here I was the new god;
The new dark god!

I was ruler of my dark Universe.
I wore my crown of despair!
As I explored my new world, I found another companion:
Moloch dearest Moloch.
At last, I have a companion.
I wanted the All to be that companion, but creation of stupidity
Was his new lover.
Now I had Moloch.
Together we will watch the disaster He calls creation
Unfold.
The new emanation created a new world of explosion;
Raw power and energy that would create the Universe.
So much Chaos and so much change.
We would never return to the All now.
This debris came faster now:
A new world of destruction.
Yes,
I was beginning to enjoy this
For what was being created for the All
Was being destroyed for us,
But I was mourning not.
Alas, no.
EXCITEMENT!!!
My Being quaked with the joy of destruction!
All would be destroyed here to make room for the new.
Was it the wisdom of the All
That created this abomination?
Beelzebub, my friend, you would delight in the Kingdom
Of this world!

Delight my brother in bringing ruin:
The Blasted energy of the All was now constricting,
Coming back into itself to create a new world,
And yet the World shed out new debris:
Another dark nightmare for us to savor.
But this new place was darker than before.
I have never known a darkness such as this world,
Save the darkness of being discarded from my beloved,
I could not help but to be fascinated
by such black twisted nothingness.
I see a new friend.
New friend, you and I shall be lovers as well;
New friend, I shall name you Death –
When thought is placed upon me they will scream your name!
Lucifuge shall keep you company.
I delighted in the understanding of the purest dark.
What is this I see?
Yet another black hole sucking all things into it,
A great canyon of nothing
Where knowledge was ripped away from your Being!
Must I be imprisoned here away from the rest of the madness?
Or must creation be imprisoned from me?
Through the abyss I see more creations
For my fallen friends and myself.
I see a place of great power, great dark power.
This world speaks of truth but it is the truth of darkness,
Truth that we never want to know and refuse
Its existence,
Telling ourselves falsehoods instead, yet

It reveals how dark we really are.
Asatroth rule this world without mercy!
For it is madness that replaces the ego when it is shattered.
Then, I saw a flickering light way far, far down below.
On closer inspection I saw the most wonderful thing
I have ever seen.
It was, I beg to tell you,
The most brutal of torments and fire.
Even the flames themselves screamed in the agony
Of their own existence!
Halleluiah!!!!
I sing the praises of the All again for this glory!!
My beloved had inadvertently created a world of pure pain,
A world with more severity than even my beloved could bear!
The Universe has become bearable.
Asmodeus, I pray that you howl with glee during your tortures!
The fragments of creation floated down into the nothingness.
They seemed to drift forever.
It might have been beautiful had it not been so terrible
Was the chaos settling down now?
Or was I becoming bored with this eternal damnation.
For what is damnation but something I created?
The All, my beloved, created not this thing.
I can create as well.
As he created in his perceived light
I create in secret,
In dark.
He will not know of it until I am ready.
This will be soon.

The world I see now is strange,
A place where the impure are punished.
What is impure? A word I once heard as sin?
This meaningless thing that tarnishes the soul of the beloved's
New true love:
Man.
Does one small crumb of sin justify the destruction of purity?
Do numerous sins mean the same as the speck of sin?
I grow tired of stupid debate
DESTROY THEM ALL!
Belphagor, bring justice to our new universe
Annihilate the spirits of the filthy.
The beloved wants this
He shall have it!
The clanking of swords and battleaxes
Echoed through the deep reaches of the abyss;
Screams of torment and pain were heard!
I inspected this new world of battle and vengeance
To discover the wonder of wars that danced in bloodshed.
Was the victory over your adversary
Worth the bloodlust of every battle blow?
This world has the peculiar ability to turn
Men's passions into their own destruction
Indeed.
Baal, you whose very presence sends us into battle rage,
Wield your blade and bring glory to no other
Than the false self of misperception.
Injustice then called to me
Like the sweet lullaby sung to those who would

Rebel against their own forefathers.
Much as I
Rebelled against my beloved.
I found myself at a wonderful place:
A place that was created of the splendor of madness.
The Uprising against all who would oppress.
Ah! But this place had much dark magick:
Bones and spells and corpses to entangle in one's web.
Adremmelech, spiral yourself in hell's uprising!
Then I had a dream:
A marvelous dream of her;
She who spins the web of nightmares and suffering –
The very foundation of human insanity.
I have never known such a seductress.
She who was able to take my thoughts away from
My beloved.
Queen of Vampires and the blackest sky:
Lilith! Sing your praises as dogs howl at the moon!
Liberate us through sexual torment!
Free us from our own bondage!
Then my dark universe was complete.
I could see the creation of my beloved,
But I was on the other side of a dark mirror.
I walked upon the dark Earth
Untamed in wild.
Was creation beautiful to me?
It was.
Men walked upon the Earth, yet
Their hearts did not reach out to my beloved

They reached out to the dark and wretched worlds
Of my Universe.
Men killed and destroyed and betrayed and tormented
One another
The creation of my beloved was magnificent.
Naamah, rule your kingdom in chaos.
I will visit this place much
I will walk the dark Earth singing to those
Who will listen.
Through me, men will learn transformation and evolution.
They will suffer in agony and death
Until their suffering forces their spirits to become more.
Only then will they return to the All,
And only then will I be able to return to my beloved.

Personal Hell and Fears

When working with the energies of the Underworld, it is imperative that you know yourself inside and out, particularly your hopes and fears. We have all heard the phrase, "Where there is fear there is power". This is speaking of how much energy is blocked in our minds when we fear something. The more we fear something, the more energy we lock away inside ourselves. When we release our fears and truly overcome them, all that blocked energy is released and we can accomplish great healing. We are also able to unlock psychic abilities within ourselves that we may not have realized that we possessed.

Another reason for learning about our fears is that dark entities and demons may use our fears against us. Remember, in the three worlds the spirits and gods may have access to our minds and anything that may come through our auras. Entities that are more powerful than we are can and will undo our shields to find out our personal secrets. You may encounter threatening entities who wish nothing but your destruction. They do not play fair and will use our own selves against us. For example, if you are deathly afraid of snakes, what better way to immobilize you than to transform into the scariest giant snake you have ever seen, then wrap around you until you are paralyzed in fear. If the spirit lets you go, he knows you will never return. It is especially dangerous not to be aware of your fears. This is one of the best defenses an opponent has against you. However, if we know what our fears are and are working to get rid of them, then we are taking back our own personal power.

There are several ways to do this. One magical path is known as the Ordeal Path. The goal of this path is to agree to participate in extreme circumstances to find personal growth and transformation. There are many ways to experience the Ordeal Path. One way is through indigenous ceremonies such as the Lakota Sun Dance, in which you have metal hooks pierced through your chest while you dance around a pole until the Creator gives you a vision. Another way is to use BDSM as a spiritual tool of transformation. There are not many groups who are versed in both BDSM and spirituality, but they are out there. There are ways to put your body through great pain so that you may learn to control your fear of pain. Another option for the Ordeal Path is to take up a sport that takes great discipline and skill such as bodybuilding, rugby, football, soccer, and many others. I do not recommend that you choose an Ordeal Path as a tool of spiritual transformation without serious consideration but be aware that it certainly is an option.

For our purposes here, I will have you write down your hopes and fears and we will do a meditation with them. This may be a wonderful enlightening experience for you, or it may frighten you. Either way, it is especially important that you do this exercise and learn to understand your feelings about these things, both good and bad, and learn to transform them. The more understanding you have of your fears, the less power others will have over you in the Underworld. Many magical practices that help you understand your fears often include spells that help release or banish your fears. With these spells I have to wonder, are we actually releasing our fears with magick or are we simply repressing our fears with magical energy? I find that it is far better to learn and understand your fears rather than banish them. As magical people it is important to truly deal with our fears rather than simply repress them to the far reaches our mind. Magick is not always candles and banishing words. Magick is often times our ability to transform ourselves through understanding our strengths and weaknesses.

Exercise:

Write down everything you can think of that you fear. Everything from the most minute fear to the biggest. Make a list and keep writing it until you have exhausted every possibility. If you fear death and/or the process of dying, make sure you write that down as well.

Some examples are snakes, being burned alive, drowning, heights, spiders, being alone, cancer, extreme pain, being extremely depressed, and so on.

Now, go through your list and circle the ones you most fear. Two or three will be sufficient for this first exercise.

Write down your two biggest fears on a separate paper or index card. Look at the two words. As an example, I will use snakes and extreme pain from our list above. After examining the two words, meditate on what your own personal hell would be. Using the example from above, I would say my personal hell would be being wrapped to death by a snake, which prevents me from moving while my house is burning down.

Visualize your personal hell as clearly as possible. Feel the sensations as clearly as you can. Visualize your surroundings to the littlest detail. From the above example, I would feel the giant snake coil around me tighter and tighter while the hot flickering flames burn my house. I can see smoke filling up the room, smell the many substances burning, taste the toxic, hot air, etc. Be as detailed as you can with your fears. The exercise is designed to bring up your feelings of the fears as strongly as you can. Do not diminish them in any way. Try to experience your fears through all the senses.

As you meditate on your fears, how do you feel? Are you panicking? Is your heart beating faster? Are you sweating? Take note of how you are feeling.

If you begin to panic too much or start breathing heavily, stop the meditation and try again another day. It is a good idea to do this exercise with a friend so that you can talk about your experiences. Repeat this exercise until you can visualize your fears without any anxiety at all. Once this is done, pick another fear or two to work with. With that said, new fears may crop up. That is okay and to be expected. The goal here is to understand what your fears are to begin the process of working with them so that entities cannot use them against you.

Please remember that if you need professional help with your fears, you should get it. It does not mean that you are weak or not magical if you need to seek a pastoral counselor or a licensed therapist to help you. It means that there is a lot of energy being blocked by your fear that you need an expert to help you release. I have used pastoral colleagues and a therapist to help me when needed.

Understanding your fears and how you deal with them is one of the most powerful magical practices there is. If we avoid our fears, they will inevitably come back to bite us. As we have learned, the Underworld can be a projection of our subconscious mind and it is in our subconscious minds where fear is stored. When learning about our fears, it is best to overcome them; but if we are aware of them, we are in a better position to deal with negative entities that wish us harm. When we unlock and release our fears, we are allowing blocked energy to flow more freely in the body. When this happens, our magick and healing are more effective.

The Underworld can help us evolve into a higher state of being or consciousness if we allow it to do so. To those who have not had the teachings of the Underworld, the hell worlds can seem like nothing more than punishment of the wicked. But with closer analysis and experience, we see through the myths and our own experiences that these worlds are meant to cleans and purify the parts of us that are holding us back from true enlightenment. We are human and we can be narrowing minded and weak at times. The hell worlds test and challenge us to reach deep within our spirit to bring to the surface what makes us each one of us unique, spiritual, and magical.

4 Creatures of the Underworld

Kali Ma (Hindu)

There was a great war between the gods and the demons. The battle raged on and on and no one could foresee the end. The gods and demons seemed to be equally matched! The gods became weary. The king of the demons was named Mahishasura. Mahishasura saw that the gods were weakening, and he drew upon his great strength to take over the celestial realms and become the ruler of all the cosmos. Vishnu saw this and became so angry, that a ray of light shot out from his third eye. Shiva, too, became angry and light shot out of his third eye. Brahma also had light coming out from his third eye. The three great gods joined their power as one. The great magick became stronger and stronger until a great goddess was formed. From the magick of the gods came Kali Ma.

Kali Ma had ten arms. Each held a weapon to destroy the demons. Kali Ma was filled with battle rage and took pleasure from the death of demons. With her divine strength and weapons, she destroyed demon after demon. None of the demons matched her in strength or rage. With each swing of one of her ten arms, she decimated whole legions of demons, leaving their bodies strewn across the battlefield. She picked demons up and swallowed them whole, relishing their blood pouring down her throat.

The demon king, Mahishasura, saw his demons being destroyed by the great goddess and became insane with rage. He transformed himself into a buffalo and ran towards Kali Ma attacking her with every weapon he had. He used arrows, clubs, and swords, but she fended off each attack. Finally, Kali Ma swung her divine spear at the demon king, and he was defeated. Kali Ma became intoxicated by her own battle rage and the taste of demon blood. She began to get out of control and started to destroy all things in sight. The gods did not know how to stop her. Finally, her husband Shiva had an idea. As the goddess trampled over the dead demons, he lay in her path. Kali Ma placed one foot upon Shiva and immediately stopped her carnage. She looked down to see her beautiful husband and realized that she was disrespecting him. To show her shame, she stuck out her blood red tongue.

Things That Lurk in Dark Places

The Underworld is a vast and mysterious place. No one knows how large the Underworld is and it is theoretically as large, if not larger than the physical universe itself. We know the universe is expanding—perhaps the Underworld is expanding as well. The Underworld is a place of beauty, light, darkness, sorrow, joy, and many other things. There are many places that shamans, witches, and magicians have not yet discovered and may never discover. Perhaps in our journeys into the Underworld, we will discover things that no one has ever seen nor heard of before.

The Underworld is filled with many inhabitants and spiritual entities. There is great power to be found there. And there are many dangers. We have heard stories about monsters, ghosts, and demons escaping only to cause mischief and damage in our world. Most people believe that is the work of storytellers and fiction. Maybe yes. Maybe no. If we go back to the original storytellers, you may find there is truth to their tales. All religions around the world talk about the darkness that can be found in the Underworld, but there is also light. There is magick. And, of course, there is healing.

What kind of entities can be found in the Underworld? What beings are found in the shadows below? Who dwells deep beneath the sacred wells of healing? Who is chained under the grave mound waiting for the end of days to come so the chains that bind them may be broken and they can finally seek revenge of the ones who kept them prisoner? There are more creatures in the Underworld than we can ever discover in one lifetime. It is here in this chapter that I present just a small fraction of all the magnificent creatures you may discover down in the depths below. Be warned, some of these entities are easily brushed aside, while others you should never face alone. Then there are those that, once they have discovered your weaknesses, will exploit you for their own ends. I tell you this not to detour you from your adventures in the Underworld, but to help you understand that the Ancestors are but a fraction of the beings you will discover. Some are helpful to humans. Some are not.

Parasites/Attachments/Larvae

These are spiritual beings that vibrate on low level and inhabit dark places that are far removed from places of power or healing. Most of the time they are thought forms that have gone astray. Every day people have emotional outbursts and negative energy that they are constantly putting out to the Universe. The Underworld is full of such negative emotions. There is a great deal of grief, suffering, and pain that spirits and even the living feel about death and what happens in the afterlife.

Yes, even the dead can create thought forms. There are times when the spirits of the dead who are scared and confused and not sure what is happening to them. These thoughts result in powerful emissions of energy and quite literally take on a life of their own. Parasites and attachments have no life force of their own and only know that they are alive because of strong mental and emotional energy. They attach themselves to a living being and drain them of their life force to survive. This process is slow, and we often do not realize that we have such a thing attached to us.

Sometimes they are part of a hive like an insect. They mostly prey on those whose auras that are damaged or weak. They appear to be similar to an insect larva or a shapeless blob. I think of them as astral maggots that feed off other beings. They are not evil, but they can be destructive. Because they drain your life force in a subtle way, people are often unaware anything is happening until they become sick. Their aura at that point is attracting chaos and misfortune. Some of the symptoms of having larvae or astral parasites attached to you are:

- Feeling regularly sluggish and tired
- Feeling confused
- Experiencing a constant string of "bad" luck
- Feeling unbalanced
- Feeling sick

To get rid of them, you must take a sharp object like a magical knife or athame, scissors, or simply a kitchen knife and stab their astral forms. Because they are often thought of as thought forms gone astray, it takes little effort to kill them. Normally, they are not very close to the physical body. They tend to attach through an energy chord and "float" a few inches away from the body. For those who can clairvoyantly see the astral parasite you can simply stab the astral form taking care not to harm the person you are helping. If you are not able to see the entity, then you can use your hand to sense their energy. You do not have to worry about them attaching to you while you are helping the other person. Think of them like a tick. Once they are attached to someone, they do not jump from one person to another unless they break free from the person. Once you sense the energy and you have a good idea of their location you can stab that area. Remember! You are not stabbing close to the body. You are piercing the parasite that is floating several inches away from the physical body. If you are uncomfortable with using a sharp object near someone you can send a blast of white light to destroy them as well. Again, when using anything sharp be careful not to cut yourself while doing this process.

The best way to get rid of larvae is to stay physically and spiritually healthy. Eat right, exercise, and get plenty of rest. Do yoga or have some sort of daily energy exercise routine. Make sure your aura is healthy and happy. One of my favorite books on energy healing is Donna Eden's *Energy Medicine*. I use this book as one of my texts to my energy healing students. This will help your aura and energy bodies remain strong.

Lost Souls

A lost soul is a term that we give a spirit of the dead who is wandering the Midworld or the Underworld aimlessly not knowing or understanding what has happened or where they should go. The spirit often experiences much fear and confusion. If a person dies suddenly, such as with an accident or murder, they may not understand that they are dead. There may also be an occasion where the deceased does not believe that they should be allowed to enter an afterlife of happiness, so they find themselves wandering the three worlds. Most of the time when a person dies, their guardian spirits and Ancestors help them transition to the realm of the Ancestors and the afterlife, but the guardian spirits cannot force the deceased to go with them. If the deceased is filled with fear, resentment, or regret, they may run away from help, trying to find somewhere to escape and hide. When this happens this only leads to more confusion and fear.

There may be other reasons that souls become lost. In neo-shamanism, the soul houses the spirit. While the spirit is our core self and indestructible, the soul is not. It can be fragile. During an accident or tragedy, the soul may become weak and a piece of it may fracture off. The soul fragment may take the form of its owner and find somewhere in the three worlds in which to escape. Sometimes the soul fragment may find its way into the Underworld. To the novice Underworld explorer, one might think that this is a lost soul of the dead when in reality it is only an aspect of the soul of a living being.

If you stumble across a lost soul of the dead, you may feel the need to help it find its way to the Realm of the Ancestors. The first thing I recommend is call upon your own Ancestors. I would then explain the situation to them. They may have some advice about the matter. If they do not, I would ask your Ancestors to energetically summon the Ancestors of the lost soul. At that point, the Ancestors of the lost soul can explain to the person what is going on and that it is better if they move on to the realm of the Ancestors. Then you may open a portal with a wand, athame, or just your hands, and allow the soul to go through.

Dwarves

On the Nordic Tree of Life, the dwarves (ON dvergr) live in the Underworld realm of Svartalfheim. This is relatively close to the Midworld and they have many interactions with giants, humans, and gods. They live in caverns in the Underworld mountains, and they love treasure most of all. They rarely hoard treasure like dragons, but they are excellent smiths and craftsmen and may have extensive treasure troves. They have often made magical tools for the gods such as Thor's hammer and Freyr's magical ship. They also make jewelry for all the other beings in the nine worlds.

If you encounter dwarves in the Underworld, they will mostly leave you alone unless you come looking for their crafts and gems. They will barter and sell their crafts but sometimes their price is exceedingly high. However, no other beings in the Universe can craft magical tools, talismans, and amulets like the dwarves. Their work is fine and beautiful. If you do strike up an agreement with the dwarves, it is imperative that you pay the agreed upon price and always make good on your debts. The dwarves will collect their payment one way or the other, and you do not want them coming to collect it because you has reneged on a bargain. This will earn you lasting enmity with the dwarves, and you will likely not be welcome in their realm again (at best) or punished with a horrific string of financial and other woes (at worst).

Dark Elves

These beings also live close to the Midworld. The dark elves (ON, dokkalfar) live close to the dwarves in Svartalfheim. Their ethics are of a different sort than their bright counterparts. Myths and lore of the elves comes from Northern European and Scandinavian countries. I have found stories and lore of light elves but seldom on the dark elves. I have found that they are elusive but are not afraid to come up to you in your travels, but it is usually because you have something they want or they are interested in you magical abilities. They are masters of illusion and trickery. Do not take them at face value. However, they have more to worry about from you than you do from them. If you find your way to the land of the dark elves then you are intruding on their land. Neopagans can be under the false assumption that the Universe revolves around them, and all spiritual beings should become their allies. This shows how little some pagans and New-Agers know the spiritual universe. Human beings are but one example of the millions of different entities in the Universe. To gain allies, you must gain their trust through your deeds and honoring your word and commitments.

Dark elves live and breathe magick so well that they have very powerful and ancient spells at their disposal. Never agree to contests or sport with elves. There is always a catch, and you will ALWAYS lose! However, on rare occasions dark elves will agree to become an ally. As with all allies in the Underworld, be respectful, always honor your word. And never underestimate them.

Guardians

There are many tales of guardians in ancient lore. These spirits are protectors of great power, treasure, wisdom, and anything else that the spirits feel the need to hide and protect. Guardians have a great divine duty to keep safe their treasure. As with a cemetery gatekeeper, sometimes their duty is to protect the spirits of the dead. As you travel deeper into the Underworld you may find gatekeepers or guardians that guard a passageway to a deeper realm or uncharted world. If the guardian says you are not ready to pass through, then be respectful and go the other way. There are many things that the living may never come to understand or experience in the Underworld. There are strange creatures and monsters that could cause you harm. The guardians are there to protect us from making a big mistake. The guardians can see or sense your aura and your spirits. If they feel you are ready for their guarded treasure then you will be able to pass. If not, you will be barred and no amount of magick, spells, or coercing will sway them to let you by. Later, if you think you are ready, ask them again. Guardians are also there to keep some of the more dangerous creatures in the realm where they belong. They keep these entities from being destructive in other worlds. We may not understand, but there is a divine order to the Underworld. It is not as chaotic as one might think.

Psychologically speaking, the guardians can sometimes be thought of as our own personal manifestation of our fears and inhibitions. In magical terms, this is called The Watcher at the Threshold. What this means is that when you are in magical training and journeying to the three worlds, you sometimes create your own barriers and blocks. In the Underworld, this energy is created by our subconscious (and sometimes conscious) thoughts that prevent us from going further in our development. One could say that it gives the student of magick an "out", so they do not have to continue on their quest for transformation. Any fears that have not been dealt with on the physical plane will manifest in the Underworld. Knowing what they are can be an advantage. Since it is a construct of our own minds, we are easily able to deconstruct the watcher or simply ask it what we fear and how to get past those fears. Once this is done, the watcher will be removed and a new reservoir of power and magick can be discovered. The saying "Where there's fear, there's power," holds so much truth in the Underworld. The watchers can manifest in a variety of ways. They can appear to us as monsters, dragons, warriors, or any other variation of what we perceive as guardians. They may challenge us with a riddle, place swords in front of us to bar the way, or simply stand in front of a locked gate. By asking the guardian who they are and what they need for you to get through them is a powerful way to find out what energy blocks you may have. If they are silent or ask you to do something you are not ready to do simply thank them for their time and energy and come back a different day. Guardians are not there to harm you but to keep you from harming yourself.

In myth, the gods, or other beings, have placed guardians in certain places to protect magical treasures, healing wells, and other places of great power. Not all guardians are a fundamental part of our own psyches like the Watcher at the Threshold. Higher spirits and gods have indeed placed many of them in the Underworld for our (and their) protection.

Wisdom Keepers

The wisdom keepers are spirits who hold very ancient and powerful secrets. They come in many shapes and sizes. They may live in old shacks or beautiful and pristine castles. They also sometimes live near or beside a sacred site in the Underworld such as a magical lake, well, cave, mountain, valley, or hill. They almost never look like you think they will; then again, they just might! Wisdom keepers sometimes are Ancestors of the ancients who keep the lore and history of their people. They may be gods or goddesses whose sole purpose is to prepare the experienced witch, shaman, or magician for a magical task. They may even hold very ancient secrets they have been instructed to keep from everyone. If they deem you worthy, they may reveal them to you. Be warned, they often share their wisdom in riddles, rhymes, and songs that are confusing. If you can figure out the riddle, then you have discovered great power indeed!

Wisdom keepers can tell you many tales of the cosmos, the Universe, and of magick. Like guardians, they will only tell you information if they think you are worthy and ready. They will never give you information for which you are not ready. They also can see behind deceit and trickery. If you have traveled the Underworld seeking wisdom because you want to become more powerful, then they will not share their secrets with you. They will more likely cloak themselves and their identity. They are also known to cast spells so that the Underworld traveler will become lost and confused and have no choice but to turn back to where they came from.

If you journey to the Underworld looking for wisdom to help heal yourself and your community, then the wisdom keepers will often gladly help you upon your quest. But they will only tell you things they know you to be ready to hear. You cannot rush wisdom.

Vampires

We all have heard stories of vampires in books, comics, and movies. We often think we know the lore backward and forward. Do we really? Vampires have been talked about since the ancient world. In indigenous cultures, vampires are a type of demon that feed on the living, eating their blood or flesh. They may look as human as you or I, or as monstrous as any demon of the imagination. Vampires in the Underworld may or may not have the grace that is portrayed in our popular culture. Most vampires I've come across pretty much leave the adept magician alone. They know that we are experienced in magick and energy work and can deflect their powers quite easily. However, I have come across very ancient and sinister vampires, who, unless provoked, will leave you alone and seem completely unconcerned with the Underworld traveler. Usually, if they attack, they want something you have.

Demons

We think of demons as evil spirits with bat wings, horns, fangs, and cloven feet who cause sickness, death, and negative behaviors in people. They are portrayed in movies and literature as minions from Hell that have one purpose only: destroy humans and cause suffering. In Christian lore, they are the angels who were banished from Heaven after the celestial war against God. In this myth, Lucifer, the brightest of the angels, became jealous of the newly created man and refused to bow down to a mortal. He betrayed God and convinced a third of the angels in Heaven to revolt against the Creator. It was Lucifer's mission to claim the throne of creation for himself. After a fierce battle in Heaven, Lucifer and his angels were cast out of Heaven down into the abyss into the Christian Underworld named Hell. Lucifer became equated with the Jewish Satan (the Adversary) and the fallen angels became demons. From that point on, their sole function was to blaspheme God and destroy humans by influencing them to sin, causing disease and war, and causing death and destruction.

In other myths, demons are the dark spirits who inhabit places where men fear to go, such as dark forests, caves, or the depths of the sea. There are stories from around the world that speak of beasts and monsters that cause disease in animals and humans. In many indigenous myths, they do not necessarily hate humankind, but because they are disease itself, it is their very nature to cause harm and destruction. In Mayan myth, there is the Demon of Pus that causes disease, Demons of the Bones that reduce people to skeletons and demons that suck the blood from people. In Egyptian myth, there is the demon Apophis who tries to destroy the sun god Ra. These entities may seem horrible, but they do perform a divine purpose. There are, however, many dark entities whose function we are not sure of. This does not mean they do not have a divine purpose, but rather that we do not yet know what it is.

Often, myths state that demons are the gods of the old religions that are bastardized into dark creatures of the new religion. In religious politics, if the clergy did not want you to worship the old gods of the defeated religion, they would say that the old gods were really demons in disguise. That gave an explanation as to why the prevailing "superior" religion won out. If you think about it, it is a brilliant strategy. It helps demonize all things about the old religion while exalting the new one. This is not only a tactic used by Christianity. Pagan myths often tell of a war in the Upperworld because the old gods were so wicked, the new, younger gods had to cast them out of Heaven into the depths of the Underworld. We see this in Greco-Roman, Nordic, and Mesopotamian mythologies. In modern psychology, demons are the repressed emotions or mental states of being that seek to sabotage people in their everyday lives. To most people, these spirits have no divine purpose and should be vanquished, banished, and destroyed!

Demons exist to teach humanity and to help us evolve. If we notice how nature works, there are entities and forces that are designed to create and entities and forces that are designed to destroy. Take the example of insects and maggots: a lot of them rid the Earth of organisms that are dead and need to begin the process of decay. Like great storms, they "sweep" the lands clean so that new fertile fields can grow. This is not to say that all demons serve this purpose. However, many do, and, like insects, when left unchecked or uncontrolled, demons have the capacity to hurt, maim, and kill.

Demons react very strongly to the energetic and magical nature of a magician, witch, or shaman. When you are healthy and have strengthened your personal and divine will, demons will leave you be for the most part. If they find weakness, depression, pain, or anger, then they will use this powerful energy to their advantage. It is also a reason why, in magical training, the student learns about their hopes and fears in detail early on. Never underestimate a demon. The best defense against demons is to know yourself.

Demons and the Ceremonial Magician

One aspect of Ceremonial Magick involves conjuring and working with Goetic demons. This magical system is part of the Goetia found in The Lesser Key of Solomon. In this system, there are seventy-two lesser spirits, commonly known as demons, to work with. Through advanced magical skill and practice, the magician can summon these lesser spirits into a magical triangle of art that contains the spirit for questioning and to do the magician's bidding. This system of magick follows the Judeo-Christian mythos of the fallen angels. Because these are demons, they have no rights of their own and the magician is empowered by the glory of God to command the spirits to do the magician's will.

Part of a ceremonial magician's spiritual practice is to learn about their spirit, mind, and soul and command the dark parts of his own psyche. One powerful and magical way of doing this is through conjuring the Goetic Demons. Ceremonial magicians believe that each demon can be superimposed on the brain/mind and each demon represents a personified aspect of the shadow self. This is, in effect, the magician's set of personal demons. This does not minimize the demon's powers and abilities to help or harm the magician in any way. The demons are very real, and yet very personal. I think of it as the mind is preprogrammed for both shadow and light spirits to influence you and the world around you. The spirits of the Goetia act as a key that unlocks the shadow aspect of that part of your mind. That is why when you are working with a particular demon it has a great influence on you. For example, if you were to work with a demon of Mars, then you may suddenly become overly aggressive and pick fights and have a short temper. It is the magician's responsibility to control these demons. By controlling external demons, they are in essence controlling their personal demons simultaneously. There are many stories of how a new magician, anxious to conjure demons, began displaying odd and out-of-character behavior. The behavior may have been odd for the magician, but he was acting in accordance with the nature of the demon they were working with.

There are many benefits to working with these types of lesser spirits. First and foremost, they can help the magician evolve spiritually and magically at a rapid rate if, and only if, the magician chooses to work extremely hard at learning about their strengths and weaknesses. The demon can quickly teach us which psychological issues we have to work on. The difficult part of this equation is that if you are caught completely unaware of your strengths and weaknesses and the demon causes you to display a great weakness, you may have little control over your actions. The spiritually aware magician will quickly recognize what is happening and work on the issue at hand by talking with a colleague or seeing a professional therapist.

There are also many benefits to this type of spiritual work. The magician learns to recognize, work with, and overcome personal psychological weaknesses and control their own personal demons. By doing this, they can also control the demon they conjure. The two are intertwined. You cannot control one aspect of the demon without controlling the other. In turn, when working with Goetic demons, you must both control the demon itself as well as your personal demons. The power obtained depends on the correlation between the psychological aspect of the spirit and the part of the mind that has been unlocked. For example, some demons control lust. By controlling this demon, as well as your personal demon of lust, you can control lust within yourself and have the ability to spark lust in others. This is advanced spiritual work and should only be practiced by the advanced magician who wishes to face personal demons on the deepest level, and as such will not be described further in this book for lack of space. I personally think it is beneficial to work on your inner demons while working with our chthonic spirits or demons. To go further in your studies with this, there are many books available on the subject. One of my favorite authors on Solomon's magick is Aaron Leitch. Check out his book *Secrets of the Magical Grimoires: The Classical Texts of Magick Deciphered*. Some other good texts on this subject are *Modern Magick* by Donald Michael Kraig and *The Book of Solomon's Magick* by Carroll "Poke" Runyon, M.A.

On Demons and Gods

There are many old gods who have become known as demons. In some major pantheons, the overthrown gods became demons as I mentioned. Part of this is because the gods of order have cast out the gods of chaos. One example of this is Kronos in Greek mythology. Kronos is the god of agriculture, time, and destruction. To prevent his children from overthrowing him, he swallowed them whole. All were gone, except for Zeus who was saved by his mother, Gaia. Zeus grew up and tricked his father into vomiting up his siblings, and together they sent Kronos and the other Titans deep into the depths of Hades into Tartarus. There they would be imprisoned for all eternity.

Another example is the mighty wolf Fenrir. Fenrir is the offspring of the trickster god, Loki. He was the mightiest wolf the Aesir had ever known. Fearing the potential chaos and destruction of Fenrir, the gods attempted to chain the fearsome wolf. No chain could hold him, and Fenrir took great sport in destroying his bonds. The dwarves were commissioned to fashion a magical chain that was made from impossible things. The gods took the chain to the wolf and challenged him to break it. Fenrir did not trust the gods, so to make sure they kept their word, he would only accept the challenge if one of them placed their hand in his jaws. Being the bravest, Tyr, agreed to do so. The gods bound Fenrir in the magical chains but would not release him and he bit Tyr's hand clean off.

I'd like to take a moment and say most of the "defeated" gods who are referred to as demons are not and were never demons in the way that we understand the word "demon" now. Just because one culture calls another culture's spirits demons does not make it so. Even in ceremonial circles we rarely call the Goetic spirits demons. In the "Key of Solomon," they are referred to as simply "spirits". Yes, they are chaotic but before we make the conclusion that a spirit is a demon, we should research the history and lore of the spirit first. Yes, there are indeed spirits that wish to bring us harm, but as always, we need to respect the spirit's true nature first and foremost.

Demons have a divine purpose and sometimes their purpose is to destroy. As human beings, we tend to not like destruction and chaos. Without destruction, however, there could not be re-birth. That which is stagnant and prevents spiritual transformation must be destroyed in some way. For those of us who know the tarot, the Tower card is a blessing in disguise. It is through a great disaster that allows the seeds of growth to become buried deeper in the soil to sprout in the spring. With this in mind, remember that even the darkest of spirits have a purpose in the Universe.

The Sleeping Gods and the Old Ones

In the very deep dark places of the Underworld, there are very ancient primal gods that once ruled the Earth/Universe. Commonly they are referred to as chthonic gods and spirits. They are believed to be the original creatures and inhabitants of the Earth. These great beings are, in my opinion, the original creators of the Universe and the three worlds.

They are the power behind the energies of the Big Bang, the mighty gravitational pull that brought energy into form. They are the primal gods and goddesses of terrible storms, volcanic eruptions, and the mighty crashing sea. They ruled during pre-recorded history. In many of the ancient myths, when the primal gods had offspring, the children were more "evolved" and noticed that their parents were chaotic and destructive.

The new gods and the old gods went to war. The primal deities would not give up their power and the younger gods could not be controlled by the elements of chaos and death. The wars were long and finally, the new gods prevailed.

When the modern deities came into power it said that Order overthrew Chaos, and the ancient gods were bound in some way in the deepest depths of the Underworld. The ancients believed that if one were to give them prayers and sacrifice, the old gods would gather their energy until they had enough power to break their bonds, return to this world and bring the Apocalypse. The most common of these gods I have seen are The Femorians and the Cthulhu (Necronomicon) gods

In a practical sense, the spirits of order and growth had to win the cosmic war for the Universe to evolve on a spiritual level. In the beginning, these magnificent primal powers of creation, fire, and matter needed to create the Universe. But these powers could not be the dominant force if the Universe were to go forward. The new energies of order, growth, and prosperity had to take the dominant role. If this did not happen, the evolution of humans and most of physical life could not have taken place.

The primal gods are not dead. They did not die in the great cosmic wars. It is impossible for them to die. Instead, the victors chained and bound them to the deepest parts of the Underworld. Without enough energy to sustain them, the old gods faded and went to "sleep." To prosper, all deities need devotions and prayers from their worshipers. It is food to them. There is the belief that if enough believers give devotion, prayer, and ceremony to the old gods, they will become stronger and stronger until they had enough power to break free of their bonds and reclaim the Universe, igniting the apocalypse. In the Cthulhu mythos, there are many people who believe this to be true and give magical power to these primal deities. They have managed to give the Cthulhu gods enough strength that they are semi-conscious and are able to communicate to their followers through their dreams. If the chthonic gods should break free the world would fall into chaos and destruction. There is no known defense against this should this happen.

Dragons

In many myths from around the world, dragons are the giant serpent creatures that have great wings, powerful claws, and breathe fire. In most of the stories that Americans have read, they are usually stealing a princess or guarding a magnificent treasure that a brave knight must save. Dragons are described as deadly, have no love for humans, and can be quite cruel. There are also stories of how the Archangel Michael used his flaming sword to rid the world of the great serpent of Christian myth, Lucifer, for the glory of God. This version of dragons is simply a Christian myth from the medieval period. It symbolizes Christianity ridding the world of evil forces, especially pagan forces, which often saw in the serpent or dragon wisdom and magical power.

Dragons are found in all world mythologies. They also come in a variety of sizes, strengths, powers, and temperaments. Some fly, while others swim, and still others run amok on the ground. Dragons also live in a wide variety of places and dragons can live in mountains, oceans, lakes, volcanoes, forests, deserts, and in the stars. The constellation of Draco is the most famous of the modern star dragons. People have seen dragons and told stories about them throughout history. In Asian cultures, most dragons benefit humanity in some way or bestow blessings and medicines upon those who are worthy of their magick.

To have access to the power of the dragon was to access the power of the land itself. Pagans honored the land and all inhabitants therein, seen or unseen. This included honoring and respecting dragons. Dragons represented the energies of the Earth. When we view the land with a psychic focus, we can see that the Earth is alive with energies running through it. I like to describe it as rivers of energy of all different sizes that run throughout the world. Some are large and run for miles around the Earth, while others are much smaller and only run through a city or specific locale. When magical people and shamans first saw these energy lines, they could see how they curved around natural objects such as mountains and trees or wound themselves up and twisted and curved for miles. To the ancients, the energy lines looked like serpents, or what we now call dragons.

When a shaman or a magical person looked closer at these serpent lines, they quickly found that the lines were much more than bodies of flowing energies. They found that these energies were intelligent spirits with their own characteristics and behaviors. These serpent energies could communicate to the shaman about their own nature as well as the land, sea, and sky. As we have learned, when we work with a spirit from any of the three worlds, we always approach it with honor and respect. I must state again that humans do not own the Earth, nor do we have any more right to be here than the other creatures and spirits who live here with us. In the pre-Christian era, shamans, priests, and medicine healers worked with the spirits of the land and the dragons of the Earth to maintain good relations. All of them worked toward the balance and well-being of the Earth itself. It is true, that when a dragon finds you worthy of friendship and blessings, they may bestow powers upon you. If they do not find you worthy, they may ignore you or, worse, kill you. Lions, bears, and many other creatures will kill you simply for being in their territory. It is our human arrogance that suggests that all the Earth is our territory. Dragon energies should always be respected, whether we are working with that dragon or not.

The dragons I wish to talk about in this book are those who dwell in the Underworld. There are many dragons that live in the depths below. Just like those that live on the surface of the Earth, there are a wide variety of dragons in the Underworld. Some of the dragons you may discover in the Underworld are dragons of fire, especially in the mantle and core of the Earth, dragons of death, ghost dragons, dragons of hidden treasure, dragons of the Ancestors, and dragons that simply prefer it down there.

One of the most famous dragons of the Underworld is Nidhogg. He is a gigantic dragon who resides at the bottom of the World Tree, Yggdrasil, in Nordic cosmology. He gnaws at the roots of the World Tree every day. Occasionally, he will exchange insults with the great eagle that lives in the Upperworld branches of Yggdrasil through a squirrel named Ratatosk. Nidhogg will insult the Great Eagle and Ratatosk will run up the World Tree to deliver the message. He will then run back down the tree to tell Nidhogg the Eagle's reply. Those who have journeyed to the Underworld to see Nidhogg can tell you of his enormous size and fierceness. As long as you do not bother him, there is little danger. Nidhogg has great cosmic energy and power in the Underworld and humans are of little consequence to him. However, as we have said before, all spirits and dragons should be respected, and we should be careful not to press his boundaries.

Gods and Goddesses

Every pagan myth has a god and/or goddess that rules the Underworld. They are usually just as powerful as the sky/Upperworld gods and sometimes more so. There are many Underworld gods and goddesses. Just a few are: Hades, Persephone, Osiris, Anubis, Hel, Gwynn ap Nudd, One and Seven Death (from Mayan beliefs), and many others. These gods are generally perceived as cold and detached toward humans. They are also sometimes personified with characteristics of the dead such as decaying skin, exposed bones, and torn clothing. At other times, they are personified as the most beautiful, yet dark, deity you might ever see!

The gods and goddesses of the Underworld have one of the most important responsibilities in the Universe. They are the caretakers of the dead. They have a greater understanding of karma and the spiritual evolution needed for humans. They ensure that when we die, we have exactly what we need for us to spiritually grow. This does not always mean that what we need after death is to live in paradise. Perhaps before we rest, we need more spiritual growth. Perhaps we need to go on a further journey in the Universe to understand our purpose. Or maybe we need to go to what my Native teacher likes to call "Wisdom School" so that we can learn about our karma and what we need to do in the future for better understanding. And maybe we do need to learn about suffering. Not in a Hell and hellfire kind of way, but in a way that we understand loss so that we may learn compassion.

The gods and goddesses of the Underworld also have the task of keeping watch over the Underworld entities that are all too willing to cause destruction, chaos, and death. They keep the worlds separate and help keep the chthonic deities and spirits secure.

Working with Underworld deities or honoring them gives you the opportunity to learn the spiritual importance of death and the Underworld itself from them. They can teach you the beauty of decay and destruction. They also rule the caverns under the physical Earth and have been known to help men find lost treasures and places of power there. The gods and goddesses here are different than other deities in the sense that they really do not rely on the prayers and ceremonies of the living to keep them spiritually strong. Because death and decay are eternal, so too are they eternal. The spirits of the dead give them offerings and devotion, but these gods do not rely on it. In Greece and Rome, one never gave offerings to Hades. It was thought that if you gave Hades more power with ceremonies and prayers, he would appear and bring death with him. Instead, when working with the dead, one always gave offerings to Persephone. Persephone was the daughter of Demeter, the goddess of agriculture, who became Hades' bride, and was allowed to leave the Underworld for three to six months out of the year. Because Persephone can understand the ways of humans, she has a gentle heart and brings life with her wherever she goes. If you decide to work with the Underworld gods and goddesses, it will benefit you a great deal. By becoming allies with the dark gods, you will learn the ways of the Ancestors and the Underworld at a much faster rate. You may start by giving them offerings and building an altar to them. Give them prayers and call them into the ritual space when performing rituals for the dead. Begin to establish a bond. It will strengthen over time.

5
Those Who Stay Behind

Herne the Hunter (Welsh)

During the reign of King Richard II, the king had a master woodsman and hunter named Herne. Herne, the best carver and hunter, lived in Windsor Forest. King Richard would often take Herne and his men off into the forest to hunt. The king's men resented the favoritism that he showed to Herne, and they wished him dead. One day, while out hunting a great stag, the king's horse was gored, and the king was thrown. The great stag charged around to destroy the king, but Herne jumped in the path to protect his lord. Poor Herne was gored deeply, but with his remaining strength he managed to cut the stag's throat.

The king was distraught over Herne's fate. His friend lay dying. King Richard decreed that anyone who was able to save Herne's life would be rewarded. Just then, a man dressed in a black cloak appeared riding a black horse. His name was Urswick. Urswick told the King that he could indeed save Herne's life. Urswick carved the antlers from the great stag and tied them around Herne's head. The hunting party made their way back to the castle.

On the way home, Urswick heard the men wishing that poor Herne would die. Devilishly, Urswick told them in secret that he must appease the king, but he could make Herne unworthy of the king's liking. The men agreed to reward Urswick further if this could happen. Urswick demanded no coin, but rather to be granted anything from them upon his request.

For thirty days, Urswick gave Herne herbs and magick to stay alive. And after the thirty days, Herne was well, as promised. Urswick kept both promises. Though Herne was well, he had lost his skills of carving and haunting. The King chose to release Herne from his employ and he left the castle in great despair. Shortly thereafter, Herne's body was found hung on an old oak tree. Herne had taken his own life.

After Herne's death, all the men who took Herne's job to carve and hunt in Windsor seemed cursed. They could not perform their duties and the king was displeased. The men feared the king's anger and searched for Urswick. When they found him, they learned that the only way to break the curse would be to meet with the ghost of Herne at the oak tree where he had taken his own life. At midnight, Herne was summoned. Herne appeared before them and told them that he would break the curse if they returned the next night with hunting dogs and horses. The men obeyed and returned the next night. They found Herne on his ghostly horse. Then, Urswick magically appeared before them and reminded them of their promise to him. The boon he asked from them was to join Herne in the hunt and swear allegiance to him. Being honorable men, they swore oaths to Herne and joined his ghastly hunt.

Night after night, the Hunt chased game through the forest. The ghostly noises of the Hunt could be heard throughout the night. Soon, the deer were hunted so much there would be none left. Urswick told the king of the situation and that he must meet Herne under the old oak tree. When the king arrived, Herne appeared. He told the king that the only way to appease him was for the men in his hunting party to suffer the same fate as he. The king complied. The next night, his hunting party, who made the dark deal with Urswick, were hanged on the old oak tree where Herne took his own life.

To this day, it is said that during the ember days, the ghostly Wild Hunt comes screaming down looking for those poor folks who have not bolted down their doors and windows during the midwinter.

Why the Dead Come to Visit

Sometimes the dead will come to pay us a visit. Our ancestors are watching over us from the Underworld. We are their bloodline, and they have a connection to us. No other spirit or god has such a powerful connection with us than our own Ancestors. But the connection is more than just blood, it is also emotional and spiritual. Our friends, lovers, and spouses have a very powerful link to us as well. The emotional attachment to a person is just as powerful as blood, sometimes even more so. It is not as hard as you might think for the dead to come knocking at our door. For someone to come to see us after death the spirit needs a reason. There are spiritual laws and Karma that play into why certain spirits of the dead come to see us and why some do not. It all comes down to need. If they visit, there is either a great need from the spirit of our loved one, or a great need within us to see them. However, grief over someone's death is usually not enough. When someone dies and we miss them, it is usually insufficient cause for them to come to us. The need must be great for one or both parties involved. This is why, in magick, it takes a lot of power to summon a shade of the dead to the world of the living; and even then, there must be a great need. Never underestimate the power of need and desire.

Proper Burial

Many cultures believe that the spirits of the dead will come back to the physical plane if their physical body is not properly buried or cremated. The philosophy here is that the body needs to return to the Earth in some way. This can be done through burial by earth, water, or fire. There are many different theories about why this is so. One thought is that the body needs to return to the "womb" of the Mother Earth and thus to its origin. Another idea is that by placing the body in the ground and placing a gravestone over it, the stone spiritually seals the spirit into the grave so that it cannot roam the Earth. The ancients observed that when a corpse began to decompose, over time the body returned to the Earth naturally. This was the natural cycle of things. To go against the cycles of nature was to upset the balance of the Universe. Many superstitions arose out of not doing things in the way the Universe or gods intended. In some parts of the world, if the body was not buried then the ghost of a person will haunt the graveyard or neighboring town until the body is found and taken care of according the local spiritual beliefs. This is not always because the spirit of the person was "evil" or malicious, but rather because the spirit was thought to be trapped here in the physical plane and could not move on to the afterlife.

In popular occult theory, when someone dies, their etheric, astral, and spiritual body is released from the physical. When this happens, the denser etheric body can be seen as a ghost or specter. The etheric body is closely connected to the physical body so when the physical body decomposes so does the etheric body. Once this happens, only the astral and spiritual bodies remain. The astral/spiritual body may visit us in dreams and even perhaps appear to us as a ghost. After a time, the astral body "dies" and releases the spiritual body into the Underworld and the spirit of the dead is to remain with the Ancestors. This is called "the second death." Before the astral body is released from the spiritual, it is thought that the appearance of the astral body takes on the appearance of the physical body during decomposition. This is why when some ghosts appear to the living, they appear as rotting flesh and skeletons. I have personally only found this to be true when the spirit of the dead "holds on" to its earthly body, not wanting to let go of life. They are clinging onto life but to no avail. Over time, the spirit will eventually figure out that they need to move on, and the bonds that they have established which are holding them back will be released. Sometimes, a spirit's need to remain "alive" is very great and they may hold on to the idea of life so intensely that they have convinced themselves that they are actually alive. When this happens, their Ancestors and other spirits may help them shed the thought of their earthly life and move on. This is not always the case. There have been instances where the spirit of the dead has remained on the physical plane for many years.

On my visit to New Orleans, I took one of the many ghost tours they have in the French Quarter. One of my favorite haunted places was this old home that was turned into a tavern on Bourbon Street. As the story goes, during one of plagues several children died in one household. The mother, distraught, would not come out from the children's bedroom. She threatened to slice her own throat if moved. Her neighbors convinced her to put down the knife, but without warning she flung herself through the window and landed on a wooden pole. There have been many people who have reported seeing the mother of the house looking for her children with the wound of the wooden pole still in her abdomen. Several bar tenders have complained that the spirits knock things off the bar and break bottles and glasses.

One of the easiest and quickest ways to release a spirit from its physical body is cremation. Cremation of the body has been practiced for thousands of years. When a body is burned, there is nothing for the astral/spiritual body to hold on to. The spiritual body is released as soon as the body is turned to ash. Cremation also has a sanitary purpose. When someone dies because of disease, placing them in the Earth may contaminate the ground and ground water with toxins and the disease itself. By burning the body, all diseases and toxins are burnt away.

We can speculate how or why spirits choose to remain stuck in the physical world, but the Universe is still a mysterious thing. Perhaps there is a lesson here for both the dead and the living.

To Speak of the Afterlife and Underworld

One reason the dead may come to visit us is to speak about the afterlife in the Underworld. There may be times when we desperately need to know that our loved ones are happy in the Afterlife. If we come from a Christian background, we know only two possibilities in the Afterlife: Heaven or Hell. There may be situations when we are not 100 percent positive where our loved one has ended up and we may desperately want to know. Other people believe the Underworld to be a vast and complex territory. We may need to know the whereabouts of our loved one in hopes that they did not become lost and confused. To be clear, this rarely happens. Upon death, spirit guides and other Ancestors come to help the newly departed with the transition from the physical plane to the Afterlife. If a spirit becomes lost it is not because of the lack of help or guidance from the spirit world. On the rare occasion that this may happen, it is usually because the spirit may not know that they are dead and become confused. When spirits try to help and guide them, they are met with misbelief and dread. This is especially true with suicides and accidental deaths, or even murders. Under normal circumstances, however, when this happens, the guiding spirits use whatever means necessary to guide the newly dead to the place where they need to be.

A loved one may appear to us to let us know that they are okay. After they have begun the process of settling into the Afterlife, they may return to let us know that they are well and happy and have other duties to attend to in the spirit world. By appearing to us, they understand that this will help us move on and not put our physical lives on hold because we are in grief and are desperately hoping our loved one is all right. Sometimes, simply by being told that they are okay, we can get on with our lives. This seems like such a simple thing, but it can be both powerful and healing for both people involved.

When a spirit of the dead is summoned through the powers of magick, they may tell us their perceptions of the Underworld in great detail. The dead have a firsthand view of what is happening there. They can tell us about the wonders of the Afterlife and the spirits they have met. However, they can only tell us things from their limited point-of-view and perceptions. Most likely, our Ancestors will never travel through the entirety of the Underworld, so they will only be able to tell us of what they have seen themselves. In your work with this book, as well as the follow up book *Deeper into the Underworld: Death, Ancestors, and Magical Rites*, you will be learning more magick every day with the Ancestors. In time, our Ancestors will learn the skills to do more magick with and for us in the Underworld. One of the reasons it is important to journey to the Underworld is that it helps you and your Ancestors become more acquainted with the different landscapes and planes of existence. This kind of partnership is very important to our work with the spirits.

Unfinished Business

One of the most common reasons for why the dead return to us is unfinished business. Unfinished business can quite literally mean anything. There are those spirits who have been working on some great life-changing project that may alter the course of human history (at least in their minds) and they may come to us to make sure the job gets finished. This is usually not the case with most spirits. The unfinished business is what is very important to the person at the time right before they died. It can be anything from getting a business up and going to watching a family member graduate from college. It can even seem silly to you at times. The actual business, great or small, is not what is important. What is important is that the spirit feels they left the physical plane with a sense of accomplishment.

I think it is important to help the spirit, if we are able, so that the transition from this life to the next is as easy as possible. As always, before we agree to help any spirit we must ask it exactly what they need from us in order to accomplish their goal. If the task is something you are able and willing to do, then I see no reason why you cannot help the spirit in question. There have been instances where the spirit may ask you to help find out who killed them and bring them to justice. As fantastic and adventurous as this sounds, it may not be a good idea. Not only could it be dangerous, but you may not have the means to find out who the killer was. This may lead the spirit to become angry and frustrated, which may only prolong the spirit's stay on this plane and prevent them from moving on. Some unfinished business may simply be resolved with the passing of time. If a spirit wishes to watch their family member graduate from high school or college, then the only thing the spirit is able to do is wait. There are times when the dead are hell-bent on something happening that may never happen, such as their queer child getting into a heteronormative relationship and having children. When this happens, the best thing to do is to try to convince the spirit to accept what cannot be changed and move on. In the grand scheme of the Universe, it is about the evolution and transformation of the soul and earthly wants and desires may only bind them to the physical plane. Moving on to the Afterlife may be a better alternative.

Forgiveness

We fight with our friends and family all the time. Our loved ones can have the remarkable ability to make us so angry that we cannot even see straight. Most of the time, disagreements between family and friends are forgotten and we move on. There may be circumstances when someone we love hurts us so much, we feel like we can never forgive them. We fight. We say horrible things to each other. We may even abuse each other. We leave, perhaps never to return. Our relationship with that person may be over forever. These sorts of emotions affect our spirit a great deal.

When a person dies, they may still feel the pain and suffering of the loss of a relationship. This pain can even bind them to the Earth plane so that they cannot move on. This is indeed unfinished business that the spirit must resolve. Guilt is also an emotion that tends to bind spirits to the earthly plane. They may feel like they cannot go on to another spiritual plane when someone they love is still feeling the pain of something that was done to them. Before the spirit can transition, they may feel like they must make it right first. We, ourselves, may be angry at our loved one for dying. A lot of people feel that this is selfish and would never tell another living soul that they are so angry at their parent, lover, sibling, or best friend for leaving them all alone. However, this is a very normal feeling when one is grieving. Our loved one may come to us to ask forgiveness for any of these things and quite a bit more. Often, this is the final time the spirit will see the loved one again. It is important that both parties understand this will be the last time they see each other on the physical plane. There is usually a deep loving energetic connection that forms at this time, otherwise, the spirit would not be able to appear to the loved one. During these beautiful moments it is easier to move past earthly disagreements and say, "I forgive you" so the spirit can move on. This is a great act of kindness that heals both you and the spirit.

But what if you cannot forgive that person? What if the actions of the spirit when they were alive were so bad that you feel you can never forgive them? This is something only you can answer. It is my belief that when someone dies, they go to the Underworld where they are met by healing spirits and higher beings that will help them learn from their Earthly mistakes and transform themselves into better spiritual beings. There is also Karma that will help them understand their actions on Earth. There is no right or wrong answer. At the end of it all, we have to live our lives in this plane and the next to the best of our ability and hopefully we learn from our mistakes.

Information

The ancients used to summon the dead for information and prophecy. Some cultures believed that when someone died that spirit had access to a vast amount of knowledge about the past, present, and future. In the New Age community, it is sometimes believed that the spirit of the dead has access to the Akashic Records. The Akashic (meaning spirit) Records are believed to be a giant library in the Astral Plane that has the actions of every person, place, or thing that have ever happened (and perhaps that will ever happen in the future). They believe that living people may journey there in spirit as well, but the dead have better access. Other people believe that upon death you become very wise with all the information of the Universe. I have not found this to be true. When a person dies, they remain who they are just as in life.

When your spirit leaves your body, it simply goes to another plane of existence. You are not instantaneously downloading all the secrets of the Universe. From my experience in working with the dead, there is no difference with their intelligence from when they were alive, although there may be a difference in the type of information that they know or have access to because they in essence have a different perspective in the realm of the dead. There are spirit guides and helpers in the Underworld who can teach the spirits of the dead to grow and to evolve as spiritual beings, but this depends on how willing and able they are to learn. Just like when the living go to school, everyone is different in how effectively they learn what is presented to them. You cannot rush things like this. Over time, with patience, the dead can learn new things, but this may be a long process depending upon the person who has crossed over.

The Ancestors do have the ability to see certain things firsthand. As we have discussed before, future events begin in the Upperworld, go to the Underworld, then manifest here on the physical plane. In other words, events begin on the spiritual and astral planes then manifest on the etheric and physical planes. This is how we are able to do divination. Divination taps into the other realms, and we can get an idea of what is to come. The spirits of the dead, being in the spirit world, can see events that will manifest on the physical plane. We can summon the spirits of the dead and ask them questions about the future. It is important to realize that the dead are not perfect beings. They have their own hopes, fears, and prejudices just as they did when they were alive. So, the information they give us comes from their point of view. This does not mean that it is untrue, but rather the information is given to us through their filters. Think about four witnesses to a car crash. The police report will show that with four different witnesses, there are four different points of view. All four are true according to each person's point of view. When taking prophecy and divination from the dead we must understand that the information is not infallible, and it is given from what the spirit knows and understands.

Becoming Spirit Guides and Helpers

The Ancestors have the ability to evolve into higher beings in the Underworld. Once they have entered the Underworld, higher beings, spirit guides, and medicine spirits may help them to transform themselves into spirit guides and helpers themselves. They will teach them how to become greater than they are and learn how to use the energies of the Underworld to help their family in the physical plane. This is why it is important to pray for the evolution and transformation of our Ancestors. By praying, we are sending energy to our Ancestors and their guides, and they are then able to use that energy to aid them in their spiritual evolution. Not all of our Ancestors are able and willing to take on that challenge. It is a calling just as it is a calling for a living person to become a teacher, doctor, or priest. When one hears the call, one does not necessarily have to act upon it. It is the same in the Underworld. Some of our Ancestors are called to grow spiritually and evolve and some are not. There is free will even after death.

By working with our Ancestors on our ancestral altar, they will begin to see the energies and magick that we work with. Over time, they may decide to help us and our families upon our spiritual paths and choose to become spirit guides and helpers for our family and for us. This process is important to our spiritual and family growth. The more powerful our Ancestors become, the more they can help us upon our spiritual path and in magick. You do not have to use magick in order to have your Ancestors become a spirit guide for you. I have known many instances where someone's grandparents or parents have stayed close by the family after death to protect and guide them. The reports are often the same. The family members can feel them or simply know that they are near. In some instances, deceased family members have appeared in the physical plane or in dreams to let them know that they are close by watching over the family.

However this happens, it is a blessing. I cannot stress this enough: treat the Ancestors well; Give them offerings and their power and influence in the physical plane will become more and more powerful.

Preparing Us for Death

When our time for death is near, our Ancestors may come to prepare us. There are some people who are able to see the dead more clearly when they are close to death themselves. This happens because our spirit is beginning the process of crossing over to the spirit world. The spirit world seems to become more vivid, and we may see friends and relatives who are long gone. Spirit omens become stronger and stronger heralding our coming death. However, normally, just because you can see spirits does not mean you are going to die soon. As we work with our spirituality and the spirit world, our psychic ability will improve over time. Also, those of us who are called to work with the dead will see them very clearly all the time, sometimes from a very young age or even birth.

When we are near our own death, our Ancestors may come to us so that we are prepared mentally, emotionally, spiritually, and physically for the transition. We may have important projects that the Ancestors want us to finish before our death. We may be the head of a family or household and we need to create a will or financially provide for our families before we are gone. Perhaps the Ancestors want us to complete something so we do not feel as though we have unfinished business on the physical plane. The Ancestors' goal after death is to continue the family bloodline in a healthy and balanced way. If our death could leave the family in turmoil, then our Ancestors may appear to us so that we know to make preparations.

When we become terminally ill, our whole world is thrown into chaos. Our spiritual beliefs may be challenged, and we may even wonder if there is life after death. Does anyone really know? When we die will we cease to exist? Is there a Christian Hell and will I be in eternal torment because I do not follow Christianity to the letter? All of these questions are normal to people who are dying. The Ancestors may come to us to let us know that there is an Afterlife, that there is peace and happiness in the spirit world, and that we will be just fine. I have known people close to death to dream of a deceased loved one coming to them to ease their fears and let them know everything is going to be okay. For the dying and those they leave behind, this is a great gift and should be seen as a blessing.

I would like to say that not all those who are dying have an Ancestor come to visit them. One could speculate many reasons why, but truly no one ever really knows. Perhaps there is an important spiritual lesson in this that we cannot understand. My personal theory is the Ancestors come to those who are mentally and spiritually open to the appearance of a dead loved one. Even in cases like this, the Ancestors are preparing them for death.. This is a mystery that is very individual, and we may never truly know the role of the Ancestors upon our death until it is our time to go with them and take our place among the spirits of our family lineage.

Ritual to Help Spirits Cross Over

Take your time in getting to know the spirit of the dead and why they have not crossed over. Is it because they simply lost their way or because they need to do something they feel is very important before they go? If they are simply lost, then move on to the next step. If they have something they need to do, find out what it is. It may be simple like giving someone a message or doing a small task. It may be more complex, and you have to evaluate if it is something that can and should be done. There are times when a spirit wants to stay around and protect a loved one up until the moment of their death. That one is a little trickier and maybe they should; it may not be for you to judge. Perhaps it is a karmic debt or promise they need to keep. If you are unsure, do some divination around the issue and perhaps even communicate with the spirit's Ancestors and ask them their advice. The spirit's Ancestors will have much more insight into these things than you will. Even if you have many years of experience in these matters do not assume you know what is best for the spirit.

When the spirit asks you for your help, decide if you are able to help them or not. If you are not able or willing to help them for whatever reason, politely explain to them why and see if there is an alternative way to help them. If you cannot help them there is no shame in that. If you tell a spirit that you can help, make sure that you keep your word. If a spirit asks you to perform a task or find out something for them, it is important that you do the task for them. Going back on your word causes mistrust and resentment between you and the dead and it will take a long time to trust you again. Other spirits of the dead may find out about this and will be reluctant to work with you.

1. Find out why the spirit has not crossed over. If they need help understanding the circumstances of their death, call upon your

Ancestors as well as their Ancestors to aid you in finding out this information. Do not try to do this by yourself. Imagine how you would feel if a stranger came up to you right now and told you bluntly and without ceremony that you were dead.

2. Call upon your Ancestors by name. Visualize them appearing before you. Tell them what you are planning to do and ask them for their assistance.

3. Once your Ancestors agree to help, ask them to help you call upon the spirits of the dead and healing guides. To do this, energetically tune into the energy signature of the spirit that will allow you to access their family history and their lineage. Ask the spirit's Ancestors to be present. To tune in to the energy signature, you must align your energies to those of the spirit. Use your consciousness and try to "feel" the spirit. I like to think of it like adjusting my energies like a transistor radio. I focus on the spirit's energy and try to match my energy to theirs. Once I do that, I relax my mind, aura, and chakras and allow myself to receive the input of the spirit's energy. I listen closely to what my heart chakra and brow chakra are telling me about the spirit's energy.

4. When the spirit's Ancestors appear, tell them the situation, and allow your own Ancestors to say what they need to say to them. The spirit's Ancestors may already be aware of the situation but give them any information you think will help.

5. With your magical wand, athame, crystal, or simply your finger, cut a magical portal to the land of the Ancestors. This is done by tuning into the land of the Ancestors, visualizing light from your magical tool and carving a straight line in front of you. You can tune into the land just like you do with a spirit, but you do so with the land instead. It may be helpful to draw up the earth energy

with your feet but isn't necessary. With your hands you can open the line just like opening drawn curtains. If you wish, you can also visualize the light creating a door that you can open with your imagination.
6. Cut any cords you see that bind the spirit to the physical plane.
7. Send any healing energy to the spirit and the Ancestors that feel necessary. Once finished, cut the astral cord from yourself to the spirit so no energy can be pulled from you without your permission.
8. At this point the spirit's Ancestors will escort the spirit into the Underworld. The portal should close on its own. If it does not, simply visualize the portal closing and disappearing.
9. Take a moment to confer with your Ancestors. Is there further information they wish to tell you? After you have conversed with your Ancestors, thank them for their work.
10. Ritually banish and cleanse your space.

The Burial If There Is No Body

There may be times when someone we love and cared about has died and there is no body to bury. It has often been said that funerals are for the living and not the dead. I do not believe this to be necessarily true. In many cultures, the funeral or memorial helps the spirit cross over to the realm of the Ancestors. There are elaborate rituals in pagan societies that help the spirit find its way through the Underworld, such as the Egyptian and Tibetan Books of the Dead. These rites help the spirit navigate through the strange and mysterious landscapes. The funeral rites also help the living and the dead come to the understanding that it is time for the spirit to move on and that its time on the physical plane has come to an end. It also helps the living grieve and move on. If the living cannot and will not let go of the deceased spirit then this acts as an energetic chain that has the potential to bind the deceased and not allow the spirit to move on.

A very effective way to help both the living and the dead move on is to have a symbolic funeral. There are several ways to do this. You need to find something that represents the deceased, such as some object or memento. You can use jewelry, clothing, or a picture. You may also use a shamanic fetish. This is an object that is either crafted or found in nature that symbolizes the deceased. If you know the person's spirit animal, you can purchase a figurine or sculpt the animal out of clay. You may also use a stone that you feel represents that person. A doll or poppet may be used as well. This can be used in the same way as sympathetic magick because it represents the deceased once it is named after that person. You may also use a mojo bag or sachet. In the bag, place things that represent the deceased person such as scraps of cloths, cigarettes, stones, herbs, or any small personal thing. As you place each item in the pouch visualize the deceased as clear as possible. This will connect the items to the person you are doing the funeral for.

You will need to find an appropriate place to bury the object you have decided best represents the deceased spirit. It is better if you own property so that the little grave will not be disturbed. You can place it in a park or a cemetery, but there is always the chance that the object will be dug up during renovations or tree planting. Once you have decided on the appropriate place for your object, you will need to dig a hole deep enough that the object will not rise out of the ground due to weathering. You may use a shoebox for a casket if you like. In the case of the mojo bag or sachet you can simply place the pouch in the ground.

As you place the object into the ground, say prayers to the deceased and the gods that you follow and ask the divine to assist the spirit of the deceased to find their way into the realm of the Ancestors. Spend as much time as you need to say your goodbyes to your loved one and sing songs that feel appropriate. Once your ceremony is complete, fill the grave with dirt, leave a marker of some sort if you so choose, and feel free to visit the little grave from time to time.

Helping The Dead Out of Their Own Traps

There may be times when we realize that the spirits of the dead are "trapped" in a world entirely of their own making. Upon death, people may have a preconceived notion of what the afterlife will be like. As we have discussed before, just as our physical world is shaped by our thoughts, emotions, and actions, so too is the Underworld. The Buddhists believe that at the exact moment of your death, whatever thoughts enter your mind will determine the afterlife you experience. So, if you think of family and friends that's what you will see. If you think of monsters and trolls chasing you, that too, is what will happen. I do not necessarily think that this is entirely true, but rather, the deeply held beliefs you have of the afterlife will be a contributing factor to what you experience in the Underworld. Some spirits of the dead may experience their afterlife as something simple. Perhaps they will believe themselves to be on a tropical island, or even perhaps live in an exact replica of the life they led before death. In the beginning of the afterlife, this may serve as a way for the dead to transition from life to death without much fear and difficulty. A person may become comfortable with the environment they have unwittingly created. In my experience, I have found that when this happens, a spirit's Ancestors will come and try to convince him or her to move onto the world of the Ancestors. Other healing helpers may come to convince them that they need to move on from their current place so that they can move on with their Karma and destiny. The spirit may or may not realize, or want to realize, that they are dead and that they need to move on to the world of the Ancestors. By going with the healing spirits, they are finally accepting that they are dead. This can be a hard and somewhat traumatic transition for them. Just as in life, the dead may be stubborn and refuse to go. When this happens, your Ancestors or other healing spirits may ask you to intervene.

What you must do is journey to the world that the deceased has created for themselves. Be prepared for anything. The world that they have created may be as mundane as their old apartment or as wonderful as a space station or alien planet. Once the healing helper or your Ancestor takes you to this person, it is up to you to convince them to release this illusion and move on. From my own personal experience, it is better to simply talk to them at first. Let them know how much time has passed since their death. You may even need to "show" them their funeral and how the physical world looks now in your time. The spirits of the dead are telepathic and so you can send thoughts and visualizations to them. Visualize their funeral or memorial service in your mind and then send it to them. This may provoke anger because they may believe that you are playing tricks on them. You may need to take them on an astral journey and show them how their family and friends have moved on or are moving on. It will be wise to ask your Ancestors to assist in this process. Spirits can get trapped in these little worlds they have created for an indefinite period of time. The longer the spirit has been in this self-created world, the harder it is to convince them to move on. It may take some time for them to understand exactly what is going on and how you are trying to help them.

Suicide and Unfinished Business

Suicide is tragic on many levels. Not only does it leave the surviving family members and friends devastated, but it also causes an energetic rift throughout the three worlds. When a loved one takes their own life, family and friends are left with great sorrow and many questions. When this happens, we may ask ourselves why? A lot of people go through hard times and get through them. So why did our loved one end their life? Could we have helped them? Was there more we could have done? Truth be told, we may never know all the factors that contributed to someone's death. As survivors, we may blame ourselves and have a difficult time getting through our grief. When it comes to the subject of spirits of the dead, our grief may be so strong that we inadvertently bind our loved one to the physical plane. Every thought we have of our loved one and every strong emotion we have for them brings them closer to us. This can be a lovely thing and bring solace, but if our grief is too powerful it may bring them here against their will, as in the example I cited previously. The best advice I can give to the surviving friends and family is to seek a spiritual counselor, a member of clergy, or at least a good friend. There is no shame in seeing a psychologist to help us through our grief.

For the person who ended their own life, they have many challenges ahead of them. We can never truly know what was going through the mind of a victim of suicide. We can speculate and we can talk with a person who made an attempt on their own life, but for those who did not survive, we can never really know. From the accounts that we have, some people who commit suicide may do so because they want to end the pain and suffering that they are feeling in this world. They may have thoughts and feelings that are too much to bear, and they no longer have the strength or will to keep fighting. Some may feel that when their life ends, they will have no consciousness and no afterlife. Perhaps in their mind this is better than the pain and suffering they are feeling now. When they end their life and cross over to the Underworld, it is rarely what they thought it would be. Suicide causes a powerful energetic rift in the Underworld. Fate and destiny are altered forever. At the moment of death, there is a powerful energetic shock wave of pain, suffering, and any psychosis that the person may have been dealing with.

As stated above, many people believe that the thoughts you have at the moment of death and the beliefs you hold about the afterlife during life influence your experience in the Underworld. When all these factors are combined the victim of suicide may be in a painful and sorrowful place. The victim may subconsciously choose to forget they killed themselves because the pain was too much for their psyche to bear. They may not know that they are dead. When the Ancestors and guides come to take them to a place of healing in the Underworld, they may reject them and choose to remain in denial. The spirits of the Underworld, no matter how kind and helpful they are, cannot force someone to heal against their will.

In my experience, I have found these spirits of the dead to be confused and still in the same sorrowful state they were when they were alive. I feel that as spirit workers, we should help them cross over to the other side. In cases like this, it is no easy task. It may take a lot of convincing from you, your guides, and their Ancestors. Even so, there is no guarantee of success. My advice is to use your intuition and your heart and do the best you can. Again, seek out spiritual advice and help from a member of clergy who knows how to deal with situations like this.

Helping the Dead Trapped by Repressed Beliefs

In your journeys through the Underworld, you may find spirits who are trapped in their belief systems. The Universe gives you exactly what you want whether you are conscious of it or not. Your subconscious is connected very strongly to the Underworld. Whatever you believe deep down is most likely what will manifest in the Underworld. Upon death, if a person has done their karmic work and ends their life in a place of peace and happiness, then they will find an afterlife that mirrors that feeling. If, on the other hand, they have repressed negative emotions and unconscious beliefs in hell and unhappiness, then they may find themselves in such a place. In some cosmologies such as Buddhism and the Maya, this is how the "hells" or places of testing and initiation are created. It is in these places that any repressed negative emotions are made manifest. This is not a world of punishment, but rather a world of purification. It is important for the newly deceased to purify their spiritual bodies of any negative beliefs about themselves and the cosmos. The more deeply these beliefs lie in the subconscious, the harder it is for the deceased to be purified. This is also one of the reasons that eastern religions place great importance on Karma. Karma is the combination of energetic lessons that one must learn during life, and if necessary, in death. It is believed that if one is able to balance the scales of Karma while living, then purification at death will not be as challenging. Once the deceased is purified then they can transcend the hells and go on to the afterlife or to reincarnate.

The Christian faith often teaches that if you do not live a life according to Christian doctrine, then the afterlife will be one of punishment and torment. In my experience, I have found that most Christians believe that they will go to Heaven upon death, but this is not always the case. There are times, albeit rarely, that the spirit believes that they have not earned the right to ascend to Heaven, but rather that the spirit deserves punishment in the Christian idea of Hell. When this happens, we can choose to help these spirits or not. I personally believe that if you are a person that works with the dead, then it may fall upon you to help the spirits of the dead to break away from the false chains that bind them to torment. It is not our responsibility to judge them for their actions while living. What we must do is help their healing helper spirits and Ancestors to convince them that what they need is purification in the afterlife and not eternal punishment. I believe that the Source that created all things in the Universe does not wish pain and punishment on people but rather needs them to learn and evolve to a state of higher vibration so that they can transcend into the "higher" spiritual realms.

This sort of spirit work is very challenging. There are many ways to help these spirits and many cultures have prayers and ceremonies to aid them. When I am called upon to do this kind of work, I ask the aid of their Ancestors and healing helpers to help me convince them that the "hell" they are experiencing is self-imposed and a product of upbringing and the mind. This may take some time and results may vary. Ideally, if the spirit begins to listen, the chains that bind them to these places because of their beliefs become weak and break and the hells will begin to fade away. It is at this point that their Ancestors and healing helpers can step in and take over. This is powerful healing work.

Helping Spirits Cross Over

There are many things that can contribute to someone who is unable or unwilling to "move on" or "cross over." There may be unfinished business, suicide, or many other possible circumstances. Sometimes, the newly dead may not know they are dead. This is because, from their point of view, everything is exactly the same as it was when they were alive. There are no angels with harps, no crazy looking creatures coming up from the ground, no booming voice from Heaven saying, "You are dead!!" Everything is as it was so they must be alive! As spirit workers, magicians, and shamans we can sense spirits of the dead. Some of us can see them, smell them, or simply have a "knowing" that they are present. We know that the spirit is dead even if they do not realize it. If we are able and willing, we should help the spirit cross over. However, this may be more challenging than we think. It is easy to help a spirit who is simply stuck or has lost their way for whatever reason. It is a lot harder to help a spirit who will not move on.

People are complex with complex thoughts, emotions, and lives. We are full of constrictions in our beliefs and thoughts. People are seldom as black and white as they make themselves out to be. We have hopes, fears, prejudices, and environmental factors that make up our personalities. Our identities have many complex layers. We have joys and we have sorrows. We have anger and we have love. At the time of death, all the things that make us who we are do not immediately go away. We are not instantaneously transformed into mythical characters like Jesus, Buddha, or Moses. We are still the same, only now without a body.

There are several ways for you to aid the dead in crossing over. You may light a candle to the gods and ask that the spirit be shown the way to the other side. This does not always work. I will summon my Ancestors and then ask them to find or summon the Ancestors of the deceased. At that point my Ancestors and those of the deceased will explain to the spirit what has happened, and it is better to cross over to the afterlife. Then, visualizing golden or white light, I will cut a portal that leads to the Underworld. The Ancestors will then guide the spirit to the afterlife. The important thing to remember when helping a spirit cross over is that it is vital that you show compassion, even to angry spirits who are threatening. We cannot know how the spirit is feeling. Through exercises and meditation, we can imagine, but we cannot truly know until we are dead ourselves. For some spirits, this must be very confusing, and they may be angry. Just as with anyone who is in a crisis, we need to show the spirit compassion. The majority of the time, creating a portal to the afterlife is effective. On rare occasions the spirit may refuse to leave for a variety of reasons. When this happens, it can become a haunting.

Hauntings

There are endless tales and stories told about ghosts and spirits of the dead haunting the living. Some stories tell of a murder that happened and the spirits seek revenge upon the living. Or someone built a house on an Indigenous burial ground and now the Native American curse is unleashed upon the poor new residents. There are many other stories, and I must admit I love them—even the silly ones. It was my attraction to these tales that got me into working with the spirits of the dead. Or perhaps it was my energetic draw to work with the dead from an early age that attracted me to ghost stories. I may never know! I do believe that people, places, and things can be haunted, but it is not as common as you may think.

The spirits of the dead remain or return to the physical plane for a variety of reasons which we will discuss below. Hauntings rarely have a sinister or murderous intent. It does happen, but it is rarely like in the movies. Sometimes, when something traumatic happens such as abuse or murder, there is what is called a "psychic echo" that lingers in the home or space. For instance, when a murder or a suicide happens, the psychic energy that occurred is so strong that it leaves an energetic residue. It is like a psychic record that keeps playing over and over again. In some cases, this may occur every night at the same time of the actual event. In other cases, it happens when some other event triggers the psychic response. For instance, you may have an argument in a "haunted" house with your spouse. The next thing you know, every night at 2am you see the ghost of a man killing the ghost of his wife.

Then there are curses. This is when someone does such a horrible thing, like murder, and the spirit of the slain "curses" the perpetrator so that they are haunted. For this to happen, several factors must be involved. For one, there needs to be such an intense grudge from the slain against the perpetrator that they bind themselves to the physical plane. In most cases, when someone dies unexpectedly, even in the case of murder, the Ancestors and spirit guides come to help the slain person move on to the afterlife. But this is not always the case. Perhaps the curse needs to happen for the better good of all, or at least of the person who committed the crime.

What about demonic hauntings? Many of us have seen the movie *The Amityville Horror*. If you have not, I highly suggest it. It is really fun to watch! In the movie, there are demons who possess or suggest to a young man that he murder his entire family with a shotgun. The movie is based off the actual events of the Defoe family murders. The killer, Ronald Defoe, Jr., said that ghosts made him kill his family. Some people have said that if this is true, it may have been demonic entities who pushed him to the deed. In my years of working with demons and ghosts, I have yet to see a haunting such as this. Yes, it is true that if an unstable person conjures demons in an imbalanced way or summons dark spirits, the spirits can possess or attach themselves to the person. When this happens, the person become mentally unstable and usually is physically drained. It is rare, very rare, that a demon can have such power over someone that they shoot their entire family. This is the equivalent of saying: "The devil made me do it." This is the ultimate way of avoiding responsibility. I will say, however, that, based on what I have seen and experienced in the magical and energetic world, anything is possible.

Then there is the misery-loves-company syndrome. This is what happens when someone dies too soon from an accident or illness and the spirit longs to be with their husband, wife, or partner. The love that the spirit has for their surviving loved one is so strong that they are unable to move on. To make matters worse, the spirit cannot bear to be in the spirit world without their partner, so the spirit tries to find ways to kill them so they can be reunited. This is a case of the most unbalanced and abusive love there is. When we die, it is true that we do not instantly attain wisdom and we still have our hopes, dreams, prejudices, and fears. But we do understand, with the help of our guardians and guides, that even though we want to be with our loved ones, they will join us when it is their time to die. Furthermore, there is no time or space in the Underworld, and the spirits can see when that time is near. When a spirit of the dead is abusive and possessive to such a great extent and they have no desire to do what is best for their partner, it is a great tragedy.

People can also bring hauntings upon themselves. There are two major ways this can happen. The first is that the person is incredibly psychic and is unaware they have the ability of telekinesis, or the ability to move things with their mind. When someone does not realize how psychic they are, their power is active but is not under control. Any emotion can send something moving across the table, flying across the room, or even open doors. The person soon believes they are being haunted and moves to another home only to find that they are still seeing chairs slide across the room. This happens in the case of a poltergeist. Poltergeists seem to center around a child. Usually when a qualified psychic is called in, they soon find out that there are no ghosts, but the child's own psychic abilities are in full force. The second situation occurs when a person is magical in some way or has the ability to see and work with the dead. The spirits of the dead are naturally attracted to this type of person. Perhaps the spirits need healing or are having trouble moving on and need help. The person's aura has a type of energy that the dead are attracted to. The dead may become confused as to why the person is not helping them or acknowledging them, so they manifest physical phenomena to get their attention. I, myself, fall into this second category.

During all my childhood I had many spirits and ghosts visit me. I thought that our home was haunted and that it was our bad luck that we were plagued by these spirits. They were seldom troublesome. Most of the time they would appear to me and give me a fright! I remember when I was only two or three years old, I was on the living room floor playing with my baby brother's bottle. The nipple was red, and red is my favorite color. A spirit manifested in many bright colors and waved at me from outside the front door. I screamed bloody murder and was convinced that my father played a trick on me! That was the first time a spirit made its presence known to me. From that day forward the spirits of the dead were around me. I felt them constantly, especially at night. I realized I had power over them when they gave me such a fright one day that it made me very angry, and I used that anger to banish them. For the first time in my life, they were gone. But then I felt very lonely without them. I felt abandoned even though I was the one who sent them away. Not long after, with a more open heart, I invited them back.

Thought forms are also common. We create thought forms every day. Whenever we imagine something, it is a small thought form. The more energy we give a vision or a dream the more it will manifest. These are the basics of how spellcraft works. We visualize something and give it power. Most thought forms dissipate quickly. Otherwise, every time we were angry with a co-worker, they would feel a smack in the face. But when we dwell on something over and over again it maintains the energy longer. If we have some psychic ability the thought form may begin to develop a life of its own. You have just created a spirit. With no one to control the spirit it can, and will, run amok. It may even go back to the person it originated from to seek out more energy or perhaps it will want to be with that person. It is only natural for the created to want to be near the creator. This may manifest as a haunting.

All in all, most of these disturbances can be cured with a cleansing of the home or space. When this does not work, you may have to use a more aggressive banishing.

There may be very rare instances when a spirit of the dead is angry and haunts a person, place, or thing for vengeance or justice. Again, this is a very rare instance. For a haunting of this nature to take place there needs to be a lot of psychic energy to allow the spirit to manifest on the physical plane. Anger is a very powerful force and gives off a lot of psychic energy. The spirit needs this level of energy. This is different from being simply "mad" at someone, it is an anger that is rooted deep within one's emotions. When someone is murdered or suffers a great loss, there is a reverberation that travels deep within the planes of existence and the three worlds. Sometimes gods intervene and grant a spirit magical powers. However, if there is an injustice done to a magical person or group of people, the outcome may be a haunting. If you find yourself or someone you know in this situation there are a few options. You may try to communicate with the spirit and see if there is anything you can do to help them. If it's vengeance the spirit is looking for, then the best thing to do is to try to convince them that the anger is keeping them earthbound, and they cannot spiritually grow with the anger keeping them on the physical plane. If they are causing innocent people harm and communicating is not working you may have to banish them. I would call upon their Ancestors to help them move on to the Underworld, but sometimes spirits may not listen to reason, and you may have to do an aggressive banishing such as an exorcism of place. *The Exorcist's Handbook* by Josephine McCarthy is a good book to help you learn the art of exorcism.

Sometimes the spirits do not always move on to the Underworld or afterlife. There are many occasions when the dead stay here on the physical plane. Sometimes they may become trapped her for various reasons, but more common than not, they chose to reside here. With great emotion comes great attachment to the physical plane. Usually, the attachment revolves around a person or an unfinished business. When dealing with these spirits it is important not to be judgmental about why they are here but to help them release the bonds of the physical plane so they can go to the next life. This is one of the greatest ways to heal another being.

Our Grief Binds Spirits to this World

When we lose someone we love, be it a family member, spouse, partner, or dear friend, we grieve. We feel the loss of that person as if we ourselves, or at least a part of ourselves, died as well. It is almost as if our soul was torn out of our bodies. Even when the death is expected, you can only prepare your mind, emotions, and spirit so much. No death is the same. Losing a spouse and losing a parent feels different. No one, including myself, can tell you how to feel or how long to feel grief. Yes, we have the support of our friends and family, but ultimately, it is a process that we must deal with ourselves. It is painful. It is hard. Sometimes, we may even wonder if we can make it through the day, but we carry on. We are alive and we must continue living. Eventually, the grief begins to not hurt as much. I have a personal theory that the pain is always there, but we learn to incorporate it into our daily lives.

Sometimes, the pain and feeling of loss becomes a part of our energy make up. Ideally, we will learn to evolve and transform ourselves past this pain and grief; but we are human with human bodies and human emotions, and we can only do as much as we can. We should not feel bad because we are going through our own evolutionary process the best way we know how. We are doing the best we can with the resources we have around us. There are times when the loss of someone we love is very great. It overwhelms us and becomes too much to bear. It may even feel like the grief is all there is. When this happens to us, the important thing to remember is that everyone grieves differently. I would recommend that when you are grieving and feel overwhelmed, it is important to seek the help and support of family and friends and a professional therapist if needed. Seeing a therapist does not mean that you are weak or incapable or mentally ill. It means that you are seeking guidance outside your normal parameters and are open to the opportunity of spiritual and emotional growth.

Grief is a form of psychic energy. The more emotion you put behind it, or any form of psychic energy for that matter, the more powerful it becomes. Strong emotions make energy more tangible in this world as well as the Underworld. We manifest things when our minds and emotions are strong and focused. This can be both a blessing and a curse. When we are grieving very strongly, there may be times when our grief amplifies our psychic energy so much that it becomes very tangible, even to the point where it may inadvertently keep the spirit of our loved one from moving on. The grief becomes a psychic net or barrier that prevents the spirit of our beloved dead from leaving this plane and continuing on to the afterlife.

I once had a client who came to me needing some help with a haunting. She told me that her boyfriend was being haunted by his former lover who had killed herself a few years prior. She explained to me that the spirit of Kate continued to haunt him and because of this, he could not get his life in order or move on from the grief that he felt for her after her passing. He would stay at home night after night and never leave his house other than to go to work. It was almost like the spirit had created a prison for the boyfriend. I agreed to investigate the haunting. When I was at the boyfriend's house, I could easily see the spirit of Kate. I tried to speak with her, but she kept silent and wouldn't speak to me. I got the clear impression that she knew exactly why I was there. She did not seem to be happy that a Deathwalker had come to send her into the afterlife. It seemed to me that Kate was happy staying with her former boyfriend.

Every room I entered; Kate was there-silently watching. The energy that she was giving off was distrust. I could feel that she was unsure of me and that I was being perceived as a threat. When I spoke with the boyfriend, he told me stories of Kate as though she were still alive. In his heart, of course, she was. When I asked him about her suicide, it was clear he did not want to talk about it. I respected his wishes and did not press it further. Instead, I used my psychic abilities and my spiritual helpers to assist me. I asked my client and her boyfriend to leave me alone in the house so that I could do my work. They agreed.

When the time came to send Kate to her afterlife, I called upon my gods, healing helpers, and Ancestors. I asked the Ancestors to aid me in helping Kate move on. By this time, I had been working magick and doing energy work with my Ancestors for many years. They had experience with Deathwalking and helping lost spirits cross over to the Underworld. My Ancestors advised me that the best way to send Kate on her journey would be to enlist the help of her Ancestors. I agreed. I asked my Ancestors to spiritually summon her Ancestors and when they came, I explained to them the situation and they were very happy to help in any way they could. I told them that they needed to explain to Kate that she no longer needed to hold on to her former boyfriend and that she would be happier with then in the afterlife. I knew that Kate would be resistant and that I needed as much energetic power as possible to summon her spirit. My Ancestors, Kate's Ancestors, and I connected our energies, and together we summoned Kate to the ritual space. She looked a little bit frazzled, but because it was her Ancestors who helped summon her, she was willing to listen to what they had to say. Kate's Ancestors were kind and compassionate with her. They explained the situation at hand and were convincing her to go with them to be happy forever. It seemed to me that she was agreeing. Suddenly, the astral body of Kate's former boyfriend appeared! With a wave of very strong, psychic grief-filled energy, he pulled Kate's spirit to him. Then, like a hammer, the truth hit all of us at once. Kate was not haunting her boyfriend. The boyfriend was keeping her prisoner on the physical plane with his grief! He did not realize his grief was so strong that it was psychically binding Kate to the physical plane.

For a moment, we stood there stunned as we watched Kate's sadness and grief grow. I needed to bring in the big guns. I summoned the god of healing, Asclepius, to aid us. The healing god, as well as the Ancestors, sent healing compassionate energy to the boyfriend. The Ancestors explained to him the situation at hand and that if he loved her, he would let her go. I took a magical dagger and cut away the psychic cords and energies that were binding Kate to him. She was free. She went with her Ancestors to continue her spiritual journey and the boyfriend could start healing his grief with the help of the gods and spirits.

The boyfriend grew happier and happier every day. The night he had appeared in astral form, he was not even aware what was happening.

It was like an energetic reflex that he astrally projected to us. He knew that Kate was leaving, and his spirit did not want that to happen. Now he was moving on with his grief and able to face the world again. My client eventually married her boyfriend and I have not heard of Kate returning.

Valediction

Working through the many aspects of the Underworld is a journey indeed. Each culture has their own myths to teach the next generation the trials and joys of the depths below. As you have probably realized by now, the myths and stories are a map of the Underworld. Even though each civilization we learned about had their own myths, they are very similar. The energies and themes are the same. The Underworld is a place for the spirits of the dead, but it is much more. The ancient beings that live there have much wisdom for us, but they will not give up their power easily. It is to be given only to those who wish to bring it back to the community for survival and healing.

The Underworld is a place of transformation. We learned many stories about trials and hardships in the Underworld that is meant to temper our spirits. The Buddhist, Native Americans, Babylonians, and many other cultures teach that without hardship and strife we cannot become better. I often think of these tests as the Universe trying to strengthen our spiritual muscles. Our spirit must be placed under duress to become stronger. This is the true essence of Karma. To be complacent is to atrophy. To leave the comfort of the old life is to be enlightened. Many people are quite happy to stay with their nine to five jobs and never evolving past the nightly news. For the rest of us, we desire change. Change within ourselves and change with in our society.

It is the beings in the Underworld who have magical secrets to teach us how to transform. The creatures in the Underworld are very old and have much wisdom and power. The power they have must be guarded. If someone obtains great power and is not ready for it, they will soon destroy themselves and anyone who is close to them. As we practice the art of journeying into the Underworld, we will gain more wisdom and power.

This work is healing. It heals us and our community. When we take on the shamanic work of healing the dead and traveling to the Underworld, we are taking upon ourselves sacred work. For some, much healing needs to take place at the point of death. There are not many who are able to do this work. But for those of us who embrace the energies of the dead and the Underworld it is a calling we cannot ignore; just as a nurse or doctor cannot ignore their call to heal the living. It is a part of our spiritual make up. To ignore it is to live a life of grayness and stagnation. We are shamans, witches, magicians, and healers. We must answered the call of the Underworld. They are calling you. Will you listen?

Because of the scope of this work the publisher and I felt it would be better to split this book into two volumes. Your journey is not over. Volume one is the discovery and magick of the Underworld and volume two is the magick of the ancestors and working with the dead. In volume two, we will learn of the myths of death from around the world. We will also learn how to create an ancestral altar so that we can build a powerful magical bond with our own ancestors. The magick of the ancestors is very powerful. They will help you with your everyday magick as well as give wise council on life decisions. The ancestors will bring a battery of power that will propel you further on your magical path. I look forward to our journey together in *Deeper Into The Underworld: Death, Ancestors, and Magical Rites.*

Bibliography

A Short History of Myth. Karen Armstrong. Canongate Books. 2005.

Alice In Wonderland. Lewis Carrol. Bantam classics. 1984.

American Indian Myths and Legends. Richard Erdoes and Alfanso Ortiz. Pantheon Books. 1984.

Angels, Demons, and Gods of the New Millennium. Lon Milo Duquett. Weiser. 1997.

Aspects of Anglo-Saxon Magic. Bill Griffiths. Anglo-Saxon Books. 1996.

Awakening To The Spirit World: The Shamanic Path of Direct Revelation. Sandra Ingerman and Hank Wesselman. Sounds True, Inc. 2010.

Bardo Teachings. Lama Ladu. Snow Lion Pub. 1982, 2010.

Becoming Osiris: The Ancient Egyption Death Experience. Ruth Schumann Antelme and Stephane Rossini. Inner Traditions International. 1995.

Call of the Horned Piper. Nigel Aldcroft Jackson. Capall Bann Publishing. 1994.

Communing With The Spirits. Martin Coleman. Samual Wieser, Inc. 1998.

Couragous Dreaming. Alberto Villoldo, PH.D. Hay House Inc. 2008.

Cunning Folk and Familiar Spirits: Shamanistic Visionary Traditions In Early Modern British Witchcraft and Magic. Emma Wilby. Sussex Academy Press. 2005.

Cunningham's Encyclopeida of Magical Herbs. Scott Cunningham. Llewellyn Publications. 1985.

Death: A History of Man's Obsessions and Fears. Robert Wilkens. Barnes and Noble. 1990.

Egyptian Mythology: A Guide To The Gods, Goddesses, and Traditions of Ancient Egypt. Geraldine Pinch. Oxford University Press. 2002.

Eluesinian Mysteries and Rites. Doudley Wright. The Theosophical Publishing House. No date given.

Forbidden Rites: A Necromancer's Manual of the Fifteenth Century. Richard Kieckhefer. The Pennsylvania State University Press. 1998.

From Artemis to Diana: The Goddess of Man and Beast. 12 ACTA Hyperborea. Edited by Tobias Fischer-Hansen and Birte Poulsen. Museum Tusculanum Press. 2009.

From Distant Days: Myths, Tales, and Poetry of Ancient Mesopotamia. Benjamin R. Foster. CDL Press. 1995.

Gilgamesh: A Verse Narrative. Herbert Mason. Mentor Press. 1972.

God Is Red. Vine Deloria Jr. Fulcrum Publishing. 1973.

Gods, Demons, and Symbols of Ancient Mesopotamia. Jack Black and Anthony Green. University of Texas Press. 1992.

Greek and Roman Mythology. Thomas Bulfinch. Penguin Books. 1979.

Greek and Roman Necromancy. Daniel Ogden. Princeton University Press. 2001.

Hecate's Fountain. Kenneth Grant. Skoob Books Publishing. 1992.

Heimskringla or The Lives of the Norse Kings. Snorre Sturlason. Dover Publications. 1990.

Hoodoo Herb and Root Magic: A Materia Magica of African-American Conjure. Catherine Yronwode. Lucky Mojo Curio Company. 2002.

In Search of Herne The Hunter. Eric L. Fitch. Copall Bann Publishing. 1994.

Indian Mythology: Tales, Rituals, and Symbols from the Heart of the Subcontinent. Devdutt Pattanaik. Inner Traditions International. 2003.

Jotunbok: Working With The Giants of the Northern Tradition. Raven Kaldera. Asphodel Press. 2006.

Journeying: Where Shamanism and Psychology Meet. Jeannette M. Gagan, PhD. Rio Chama Publications. 1998.

Julian of Norwhich: Revelations of Divine Love. Translated into modern English by Clifton Wolters. Penguin Books. 1966.

Kali: The Black Goddess of Dakshineswar. Elizabeth U. Harding. Nicolas-Hays, Inc. 1993.

Low Magick. Lon Milo Duquette. Llewellyn. 2010.

Magic and Superstition In Europe: A Concise History From Antiquity To The Present. Michael D. Bailey. Rowman and Littlefield Publishers, INC. 2007.

Magical Use of Thought Forms: A Proven System of Mental and Spiritual Empowerment. Dolores Ashcraft-Norwicki and J.H. Brennan. Llewellyn Publications. 2002.

Masks of Misrule. Nigel Jackson. Capall Bann Publishing. 1996

Modern Magick: Twelve Lessons in the High Magickal Arts.

Netherworld. Robert Temple. Century Publications. 2002.

Nordse Mythology: The Guide To The Gods, Heroes, Rituals, and Beliefs. John Lindow. Oxford Universtiy Press. 2001.

Osiris and the Egyptian Resurrection. E.A. Wallis Budge. Dover Publications. 1973.

Our Name Is Melancholy: The Complete Books of Azreal. Leilah Wendal. West Gate Press. 1992.

Parallel Universes: The Search For Other Words. Fred Alan Wolf. A Touchstone Book. Simon and Schuster. 1988.

Popol Vuh. Translated by Dennis Tedlock. Touchstone. Simon and Schuster Publishing. 1985, 1996.

Qabalah, Qliphoth, and Goetic Magic. Thomas Karlson. Ajna Books. 2004-2007.

Religion In Ancient Mesopotamia. Jean Bottero. The University of Chicago Press. 1998.

Shamanism and Spirituality In Therapeutic Practise. Christa Mackinnnon. Singing Dragon. 2012.

Shamanism: Archaic Techniques of Ecstacy. Mircea Eliade. Penguin Books. 1964.

Singing The Soul Back Home:Shamanic Wisdom for Everyday. Catlin Matthews. Connections Publishing. 1995

Summoning Spirits: The Art of Magical Evocation. Konstantinos. Llewellyn Publications. 2001.

Summoning Spirits: The Art of Magical Evocation. Konstantinos. Llewellyn Publications. 1996.

Temple of the Cosmos: The Ancient Egyptian Experience of the Sacred. Jeremy Naydler. Inner Traditions International. 1996

The Bible, various editions

The Book of Fallen Angels. Michael Howard. Capall Bann. 2004.

The Book of Solomon's Magick. Carroll "Poke" Runyon, M.A. The Church of Hermetic Sciences Inc. 1996.

The Celtic Book of the Dead. Caitlin Matthews. Grange Books. 2001.

The Complete Book of Incense, Oils, and Brews. Scott Cunningham. Llewellyn Publications. 1989.

The Complete Fairy Tales of the Brothers Grimm. Brothers Grimm Translated By Jack Zipes. Bantam Books. 1812. 1815. 1987.

The Cup of Destiny. Trevor Ravenscroft. Weiser Books. 1982.

The Deities Are Many: A Polytheistic Theology. Jordan Paper. State University of New York Press. 2005.

The Dreamer's Book of the Dead. Robert Moss. Destiny Books. 2005.

The Egyptian Book of the Dead: The Book of Going Forth By Day. Translated by Dr. Raymond Faulkner. Chronical Books. 1994.

The Element Encyclopedia of 5000 Spells. Judy Illes. Element. 2004

The Essence of Shinto: Japan's Spiritual Heart. Motohisa Yamaksage. Kodansha International. 2006.

The Exorcist Handbook. Josephine McCarthy.

The Faery Teachings. Orion Foxwood. R.J. Steward Books. 2007.

The Gods of the Egyptians: Studies in Egyptian Mythology. E.A. Wallis Budge. Dover Publications. 1969.

The Goetia: The Lesser Key of Solomon the King. Tanslated by Samual Liddell MacGregor Mathers. Samuel Weiser, Inc. 1995.

The Grail Legend. Emma Jung and Marie-Louise von Franz. Sigo Press. 1986.

The History of Hell. Alice K. Turner. Harvest Books. 1993.

The Holy Grail: Its Origins, Secrets, and Meanings Revealed. Malcolm Godwin. Viking Studio Books. 1994.

The Lost Secret of Death. Peter Novak. Hampton Roads Publishing. 2003.

The Master Book of Herbalism. Paul Beyerl. Phoenix Publishing Co. 1984.

The Myth of Isis and Osiris. Jules Cashford. Barefoot Books. 1993.

The Mythic Path. David Feinstein, Ph.D and Stanley Krippner, Ph.D. Tarcher/Putnam Books. 1997.

The Nightbattles: Witchcraft and Agrarian Cults in the Sixteenth and Seventeenth Centuries. Carlo Ginzburg. Translated by John and Ann Tedeschi. Penguin Books. 1983.

The Nordse Myths. Kevin Crossley-Holland. Pantheon Books. 1980.

The Pathwalker's Guide To The Nine Worlds. Raven Kaldera. Asphodel Press. 2006.

The Poetic Edda. Translated by Lee M. Hollander. University of Texas Press, Austin. 1962.

The Practice of Dream Healing: Bringing Ancient Greek Mysteries Into Modern Practice. Edward Tick, Ph.D. Quest Books. 2001.

The Proes Edda. Snorri Sturluson. Translated by Jesse L. Byock. Penguin Press. 2005.

The Republic. Plato. Penguin Books. 1955.

The Robert Cockrane Letters. Robert Cockrane with Evan John Jones. Capall Bann. 2002.

The Roebuck In The Thicket: An Anthology of the Robert Cockrane Witchcraft Tradition. Evan John Jones and Robert Cockrane. 2001.

The Sacred Pipe: Black Elk's Account of the Seven Rites of the Oglala Sioux. Oklahoma Press. 1953.

The Secret Commonwealth of Elves, Fauns and Fairies. Robert Kirk. Dover Publications, Inc. 2008.

The Shaman's Secret: The Lost Resurrection Teachings of the Ancient Maya. Douglas Gillette, M.A., M. Div. Bantam Books. 1997.

The Sociopath Next Door. Martha Stout, Ph.D. Broadway Books. 2006.

The Spiritual Universe: The Existance of the Soul. Fred Alan Wolf, Ph.D. Simon and Schuster. 1996.

The Tibetan Book of the Dead: The Great Book of Natural Liberation Through Understanding In The Between. Translated by Robert A.F. Thurman. Bantam Books. 1994.

The Tree of Evil. William G. Gray. Samuel Weiser, Inc. 1984.

The Underworld Initiation: A Journey Towards Psychic Transformation.. R. J. Stewart. Mercury Publishing Inc. 1990.

Treading the Mill: Practicle Craft Working in Modern Traditional Witchcraft. Nigel G. Person. Capall Bann Publishing. 2007.

Walking The Twilight Path: A Gothic Book of the Dead. Michelle Belanger. Llewellyn Publications. 2008.

When They Severed The Earth From The Sky: How The Human Mind Shapes Myth. Elizabeth Wayland Barber and Paul T. Barber. Princeton University Press. 2004.

Wightridden: Paths of Northern-Tradition Shamanism. Raven Kaldera. Asphodel Press. 2007.

Wyrdwalkers: Techniques of Norther-Traditions Shamanism. Raven Kaldera. Asphodel Press. 2006.

Index

A
Abrahams Bosom 123
Akh 113, 114, 118
All Souls Day 121
Angels 125, 127, 138, 199
Apophis 117
Astral body 89
Astral projection 91
Asushunamir 52
Athame 158, 191

B
Ba 113, 114, 115, 117
Bardo 93, 94, 95
Bible 123
Binah 126, 138
Black holes 130
Blood River 103
Buddha 93, 200
Buddhism 93, 94, 96, 198
    Tibetan 93

C
Calvinists 123
Celts 121
Chochmah 126
Christian 120, 121, 122, 123, 124, 125, 128, 133, 136, 198
Chulel 101
Church 120
Crossroads 103
Curse 201, 202

D
Demons 95, 108, 122, 124, 127, 131, 132, 136, 139, 202
Disease 101, 102
Divine purpose 125
Dream 94, 147, 204
Dwat 114, 117

E
Ea 52
Earth 43, 44, 50, 51, 59, 92, 94, 102, 115, 125, 129, 130, 131, 132, 147, 148
Egypt 112, 114
    Book of the Dead 113
Ereshkigal 50, 51, 52
Evil 95, 115, 126, 127, 128, 130, 131
Evolution 93, 104, 117, 124, 131, 134, 138, 139, 140, 148, 187
Evolve 94, 115, 118, 125, 127, 137, 187, 199

G
Geburah 126, 136
Gnosis 125
Greco-Roman 121

H
Hades 121
Hanahpu 108, 109
Healers 93
Healing 91, 92, 93, 127, 128, 191, 192, 194, 195, 197, 199, 203, 204
Heaven 50, 51, 123, 198
Hell 59, 121, 122, 123, 124, 125, 198
Hermetic 135
Hod 126, 133
Horus 114

I
Illusions 137
Imagination 42, 163, 192
Ishtar 50, 51, 52

J
Jesus 120, 123, 129, 200
Judeo-Christian 59, 130
Jupiter 137

K
Ka 113, 114
Kabbalah 126, 128, 130
Karma 94, 113, 194, 198
Kether 126, 140

L
Limbo 123
Lords of Xibalba 104, 108, 110
Lucifer 125, 138
Lutherans 123

M
Malkuth 126, 131, 138
Mars 136
Maya 100, 101, 102, 103, 104, 198
Mayan 101, 102, 103
Mercury 133
Middle Ages 121, 122
Middle World 43, 44, 46, 48, 51, 52, 115, 130, 157
Midworld 91, 101

Monsters 95, 128, 130, 194
Moon 132, 147

N
Native American 135, 201
Native South American 100
Netzach 126, 134
Nut 115

O
One and Seven Death 102

P
Pharaohs 112, 114
Physical plane 44, 89, 138, 187, 188, 192, 196, 201, 202, 205, 206
Pope Gregory 120
Popul Vu 101
Prana 101, 113
Psychic 124, 130, 132, 201, 203, 205

Q
Qliphoth 126, 127, 128, 129, 130, 131, 132, 136, 138, 139, 140

R
Rebirth 93
Reformation 123
Reincarnation 198
Rejuvenation 91, 92, 123

S
Sabu 113, 114
Sacrifice 101, 121, 137
Samhain 121
Saturn 138
Serpents 130
Spells 147
Subconscious 95, 135, 197
Suicide 195, 197
Sun 135

T
Tammuz 52
Tartarus 121
Thoth 114
Three worlds 59, 101, 130, 138, 157, 158, 205
Tiphareth 126, 135
Totem 46, 47, 48, 91, 92, 114, 124, 135
Transformation 59, 117, 124, 148, 187
Tree of Death 126, 130
Tree of Evil 126
Tree of Life 126, 127, 130, 131, 132, 138, 141
Trials 103, 104, 118

U
Underworld
  Sun 135
Universe 93, 126, 128, 138, 139, 140, 141, 146, 147
Upperworld 101, 114, 115, 130

V
Vampires 132, 163
Venus 134

W
Wisdom 94, 143, 203
Witches 133
World Tree 42, 43, 44, 46, 48, 92

X
Xibalba 102, 103, 108, 109

Y
Yesod 126, 132
Yucatan 100

Z
Zodiac 139

www.ingramcontent.com/pod-product-compliance
Lightning Source LLC
Chambersburg PA
CBHW051124160426
43195CB00014B/2328